I0813318

GATE OF HEAVEN

GATE OF HEAVEN

REFLECTIONS ON MARY, THE MOTHER OF GOD

Edited by Matthew Becklo

Published by Word on Fire, Elk Grove Village, IL 60007

Printed in Italy

Cover design, typesetting, and interior art direction by Nicolas Fredrickson and Cassie Bielak

Interior images from Alamy. Federico Barocci, *Annunciation*, 1584–1588 (p. 2); Federico Barocci, *Virgin and Child on a Cloud*, 1581 (p. 58); Charles David, *The Descent from the Cross* (After Federico Barocci), 1615–1631 (p. 104); Federico Barocci, *Vision of Saint Francis*, 1581 (p. 146).

ISBN: 978-1-68578-218-4

Library of Congress Control Number: 2024952425

Contents

IV. Queen of Heaven

The Rosary with Bishop Robert Barron

Additional Marian Prayers

Notes

Foreword

Sally Read

In the Carmelite church near to where I live, a group prays the Rosary before the start of Mass each day. For a prayer of so many words, the Rosary seems to bring on silence: the church as a whole becomes focused, my own mind becomes quieted and clear. After the Mass, a song is always sung to the Blessed Virgin, and congregants pause at a statue of her before drifting out of the door. Between that Rosary and the prayerful pause at her statue, we often hear little of Mary, and yet her presence, her silence, seems to hold us and all that we participate in: the Liturgy of the Word, the sacrifice at the altar, the reception of our Lord.

Mary's silence, and this sense of being held by her, is mysterious. As a poet, silence is very important to me—which I think is part of my fascination with Mary. Silence, in both poetry and prayer, is the ground needed for growth. Recently in Rome, I came upon a new icon of the Virgin that, for me, captures Mary's contemplative nature: *La Vergine del Silenzio* (The Virgin of Silence).[1] In this icon, the Mother of God, in

1. Commissioned by Fr. Emiliano Antenucci and written by the Benedictine nuns on the Island of San Giulio on Lake Orta in northwestern Italy. A copy of the icon

a crimson mantle, holds her left hand up as though to halt us, and her right index figure to her lips as if to say, "Shh!"

"She's telling you to keep quiet," the Roman store owner told me with a cackle when I bought a small copy for my desk. Mary, after so many years of me wondering what her presence really means in the Church, was teaching me to listen.

Already—in this silence—I hear the voices of both believers and nonbelievers crying, "But Mary hardly features in Scripture! Why do you give her so much importance?"

Again, we're invited by the Virgin of Silence to listen: all through the Bible, Mary is hiding, silently, in plain sight. She is the snake-stomper of Genesis 3:15. She stands, waiting in the shadows, as Ruth says, "Why have I found favor in your sight?" (Ruth 2:10), prefiguring the words of the angel to Mary (Luke 1:30). Mary's spirit flickers through God's choice to crush evil "by the hand of a woman" named Judith (9:10), who is "the glory of Jerusalem" blessed "above all other women on earth" (15:9, 13:18), and through Esther's role as intercessor for the Jewish people (as Mary intercedes for mankind). She echoes Hannah's song of praise—"My heart exults in the Lord; my strength is exalted in my God" (1 Sam. 2:1)—in her own Magnificat (Luke 1:46–55). But Mary isn't some pale reminder of those who've gone before her. She's their fulfillment: God's helpmate in the Incarnation of his Son. She is our Mother given to us

---

was given to Pope Francis, and it hangs on a wall near his private study where everyone who comes to visit him will pass by it.

from the cross (John 19:27), and is at this moment laboring in heaven (Rev. 12:2). Her presence fills the whole of Scripture from beginning to end—and often she is silent.

Mary's few words at the Annunciation are vital. Her Magnificat is joyful. Her words at Cana are weighted with meaning. But as the shepherds came to adore her child, she "treasured all these words and pondered them in her heart" (Luke 2:19), and when she found her twelve-year-old teaching in the temple, she did much the same (Luke 2:51).

What does this wordlessness mean? That she's bland? Inoffensive? Submissive? Again, the strength of that hand saying, "Slow down," that finger saying, "Shh." Mary's silence is about the deepest wisdom. It was only when I read a quotation by Theodotus of Ancyra saying that the Annunciation was an act of *hearing* that I began to understand our Mother.[2] It was the ground of her ceaseless prayer, her fertile attention to God, that allowed her to conceive Christ. It was only when I contemplated Michelangelo's *Pietà* that I felt her *receptivity*: I saw how Mary cradled the Son, received him from the cross, with the silent surrender of prayer. Michelangelo made Mary much larger than Jesus so that she could, physically, cradle him. But anyone who's looked with attention on this sculpture knows that she's holding more than a dead body on her lap: she's holding the will of God. She's there as he's born into the world;

2. Theodotus of Ancyra, homily 4, *In Deiparum et Simeonem*, 2 (Patrologia Graeca 77, 1392CD), quoted in Hans Urs von Balthasar and Joseph Ratzinger, *Mary: The Church at the Source*, trans. Adrian Walker (San Francisco: Ignatius, 2005), 72.

she's there as he departs it. She's there now, with him in heaven. It's this lap that we're all in as we attend Mass, connected to the silence of her listening at the Annunciation and the silence of her faith as she took the dead Christ into her arms.

The depth of that silence lends itself to the writings contained in this book. For Catherine of Siena, Mary is "Temple of the Trinity."[3] For Gerard Manley Hopkins, she is like "the air we breathe."[4] Before I discovered that Mary is seen as the shoot that will bring forth Christ (Isa. 11:1) and read Hildegard of Bingen's description of her as a "branch,"[5] I, too, was writing about Mary as a tree: "the deep roots" beneath her son.[6] In her school of silence, I began to understand that a tree suggests Mary because she's from the earth and reaches up to heaven—and in the family tree of salvation, she's the branch that sprouts our Savior! This makes her link to God unique—and his to her. The Christ child can hold onto nothing but her face "like a constellated sky," and she has "no lights but [his] eyes."[7] Which makes her, also, the model of how we should love Christ and let him love us. Without Mary's unsurpassable human witness, without the resounding of Christ's joy and pain in her, his life and death would risk, far more, our indifference and forgetfulness. There is no indifference and forgetfulness in

---

3. See page 52.
4. See page 21.
5. See page 4.
6. See page 105.
7. See page 59.

Mary: she holds everything in the silence of her heart.

Swallowing the flesh of Christ, of course, brings on the greatest silence of all. It's difficult to think angry or unpleasant thoughts in those moments of Communion. We're caught in the arms of the Beloved, and there's no need for words. Christ in the Eucharist sees us (or lets us see that he sees us) in a remarkable way. He takes us to the inner recesses of ourselves where, in that encounter, there's nothing but him and our own listening. Often, my problems seem to dissolve. I'm reminded that my venial sins are burnt up when I receive his Flesh. For those first few moments—before I go out the door and collide with the world again—I'm straightened out, touched by the divine.

As I leave the church and go for my evening walk by the sea, I think about Mary, and the fact that she was the first to have Christ within her body—not as we do, in the form of the Host, but as a growing child who fed from her, who needed her, who carried his mother's cells within him just as she carried his. What transformation, what divinization, must she have gone through. Thomas Aquinas wrote that things are hotter the nearer they approach what is hottest, and therefore, we become more like God the closer we move to him.[8] We can only imagine the intensity of the fire that sustains, illuminates, and transforms the Blessed Virgin.

8. Thomas Aquinas, *Summa theologiae* 1.2.3.

I have long wanted a book like this—not only to remind me and explain to me Marian teaching but also to bring together in one place poetry and reflections about the Mother of God. Mary wrote nothing down. Her words in Scripture are few. But if we're familiar with the richness of Mary's essence—which is what this book so beautifully explicates—we're going to be brought even closer to her son.

I.
Daughter *of* Zion

✴ What the Sparrow Saw—*Annunciation*

Sally Read

In the long afternoon, dull with expected sunlight,
is it possible that a bird nearby would not be changed,
at its scorched wingtip or in its jagged gaze,
by what it witnessed? Would it have seen the angel,
or just the staggered girl holding her own hands?
Would she have been so still that he rested
for a moment on her arm (like a winter branch, but soft)?
Or would he have jittered, flitted at the immense bodiless
made present (like a sunset on the doorstep,
a tsunami in the barn)? And if his breast feathers
were warmed, shaken harder by his miniscule heart;
if his eyes contained, then, a moment's intense knowledge
at what was near, or even a crazed bird-madness,
what deep hope for me as I kneel before your Presence?

The New Eve

Poem

St. Hildegard of Bingen
"O Virga ac Diadema"

O branch and diadem,
in royal purple clad,
who in your cloister strong
stand like a shield:

You burst forth blooming
but with buds
quite different than Adam's progeny—
th'entire human race.

Hail, O hail! For from your womb
came forth another life
that had been stripped by Adam from his sons.

O bloom, you did not spring
from dew nor from the drops of rain,
nor has the windy air flown over you; but radiance
divine has brought you forth upon

that noblest bough.
O branch, your blossoming
God had foreseen within the first
day of his own creation.

And by his Word he made
of you a golden matrix,
O Virgin, worthy of our praise.

How great in strength
is that man's side,
from which God brought the form of woman forth,
a mirror made
of his own every ornament,
and an embrace
of his own every creature.

The heavens' symphony resounds,
And all the earth in wonder stares,
O Mary, worthy of our praise,
for God has loved you more than all.

O cry and weep!
How deep the woe!
What sorrow seeped with guilt
into our womanhood

because the serpent hissed his wicked plan!
That woman, whom God made to be
the mother of the world,
had pricked her womb
with the wounds of ignorance,
and offered to her offspring
the full inheritance of grief.

But, O dawn,
forth from your womb has come the sun anew;
the guilt of Eve he's washed away
and through you offered humankind a blessing
even greater than the harm that Eve bestowed.

O Lady Savior,
who offered to the human race a light
anew: together join the members of your Son
into the heavens' harmony.

Scripture

Genesis 3:13–15

Then the Lord God said to the woman, "What is this that you have done?" The woman said, "The serpent tricked me, and I ate." The Lord God said to the serpent,

"Because you have done this,

cursed are you among all animals
and among all wild creatures;
upon your belly you shall go,
and dust you shall eat
all the days of your life.
I will put enmity between you and the woman,
and between your offspring and hers;
he will strike your head,
and you will strike his heel."

Reflection

Bishop Barron

Catholicism

One day, early in the first century, in a hovel in the little Galilean town of Nazareth, an angel appeared to a young Israelite girl who was perhaps no more than fourteen or fifteen years old, and they had a rather extraordinary conversation. The angel greeted her: "Greetings, favored one! The Lord is with you" (Luke 1:28). As is invariably the case when an angel makes an appearance, the girl was afraid. "Do not be afraid," the angel told her, "for you have found favor with God. And now, you will conceive in your womb and bear a son, and you will name him Jesus" (Luke 1:30–31). When she wondered how this would be possible, since she had had no sexual experience, the angel explained, "The Holy Spirit will come upon you, and the power of the Most High will overshadow you; therefore the child to be born will be holy; he will be called Son of God" (Luke 1:35). And the girl responded to this overwhelming message with utter simplicity: "Here am I, the servant of the Lord; let it be with me according to your word" (Luke 1:38). With that the angel departed.

This young Israelite woman has beguiled the finest poets of the West, from Dante to T.S. Eliot; she has been the subject of paintings by the greatest masters, from Fra Angelico and Michelangelo to Rembrandt and El Greco; over the centuries, millions of people have visited her shrines seeking her aid and calling out to her, their mother. She is referred to as the Queen of All Saints, the Queen of Angels, and the Queen of Heaven. And she has been invoked, over and over again, across the centuries, in the words of the simplest and most beautiful prayer in the Catholic tradition: the Hail Mary.

Why has she had this staggering impact? The best answer is found in the angelic encounter, in which the essence of the biblical drama is distilled. We see the nature of God on display in the graceful, nonviolent manner of the invitation. In story after story from the mythological tradition, we note that when the gods intervene in human affairs, they do so violently, interruptively, in the manner of a rape. But in the sweet invitation of the angel at the Annunciation, something altogether different is on display. Mary's freedom and dignity are respected, and her curiosity is encouraged; she is, if I can put it this way, courted by the heavenly messenger.

We also see a human being in full in the Virgin Mary. The Church Fathers were eager to contrast Mary, the Mother of God, with Eve, the mother of all the living. Barely grasping the full extent of what this surrender would entail, Mary nevertheless says she is "the servant of the Lord." And in obediently adding, "Let it be with me according to your word," she reversed the grasping disobedience of Eve. This is why medieval illustrators and commentators—so in love with the parallels, rhymes, and echoes within the Bible—imagined the *Ave* ("Greetings") of the angel reversing Eva (Eve). On the basis of the angel's greeting, *Kecharitomene*, Mary has been called "full of grace" (*charis* is the Greek for "grace"), and this means, basically, that she is someone who is profoundly disposed to receive gifts. In this, she becomes the New Eve, the mother of all those who would be reborn by being receptive to God's life as a gift.

Catechism

487–488

What the Catholic faith believes about Mary is based on what it believes about Christ, and what it teaches about Mary illumines in turn its faith in Christ.

"God sent forth his Son," but to prepare a body for him (Gal. 4:4; Heb. 10:5), he wanted the free co-operation of a creature. For this, from all eternity God chose for the mother of his Son a daughter of Israel, a young Jewish woman of Nazareth in Galilee, "a virgin betrothed to a man whose name was Joseph, of the house of David; and the virgin's name was Mary" (Luke 1:26–27):

> The Father of mercies willed that the Incarnation should be preceded by assent on the part of the predestined mother, so that just as a woman had a share in the coming of death, so also should a woman contribute to the coming of life.[1]

Throughout the Old Covenant the mission of many holy women *prepared* for that of Mary. At the very beginning there was Eve; despite her disobedience, she receives the promise of a posterity that will be victorious over the evil one, as well as the promise that she will be the mother of all the living (see Gen. 3:15, 20). By virtue of this promise, Sarah conceives a son in spite of her old age (see Gen. 18:10–14, 21:1–2). Against all human expectation God chooses those who were considered powerless and weak to show forth his faithfulness to his promises: Hannah, the mother of Samuel; Deborah; Ruth; Judith and Esther; and many other women (see 1 Cor. 1:17; 1 Sam. 1). Mary "stands out among the poor and humble of the Lord, who confidently hope for and receive salvation from him. After a long period of waiting the times are fulfilled in her, the exalted Daughter of Sion, and the new plan of salvation is established."[2]

---

1. *Lumen Gentium* 56; see *LG* 61.
2. *LG* 55.

Reflection

St. Irenaeus of Lyons

Against Heresies

Mary the Virgin is found obedient, saying, "Here am I, the servant of the Lord; let it be with me according to your word" (Luke 1:38). But Eve was disobedient; for she did not obey when as yet she was a virgin. And even as she, having indeed a husband, Adam, but being nevertheless as yet a virgin, . . . having become disobedient, was made the cause of death, both to herself and to the entire human race; so also did Mary, having a man betrothed [to her], and being nevertheless a virgin, by yielding obedience, become the cause of salvation, both to herself and the whole human race. . . . The knot of Eve's disobedience was loosed by the obedience of Mary. For what the virgin Eve had bound fast through unbelief, this did the virgin Mary set free through faith.

Prayer

St. Sophronius

Sermon

Hail full of grace, the Lord is with you. On your account joy has not only graced men, but is also granted to the powers of heaven.

Truly, *you are blessed among women.* For you have changed Eve's curse into a blessing; and Adam, who hitherto lay under a curse, has been blessed because of you.

Truly, you are blessed among women. Through you the Father's blessing has shone forth on mankind, setting them free of their ancient curse.

Truly, you are blessed among women, because through you your forebears have found salvation. For you were to give birth to the Savior who was to win them salvation.

Truly, you are blessed among women, for without seed you have borne, as your fruit, him who bestows blessings on the whole world and redeems it from the curse that made it sprout thorns.

Truly, you are blessed among women, because, though a woman by nature, you will become, in reality, God's mother.

Amen.

It was fitting then in God's mercy that, as the woman began the *destruction* of the world, so woman should also begin its *recovery*, and that, as Eve opened the way for the fatal deed of the first Adam, so Mary should open the way for the great achievement of the second Adam.

—ST. JOHN HENRY NEWMAN

She Who Is in Labor

Poem

St. Teresa Benedicta of the Cross (Edith Stein)
From "Conversation at Night"

Before the cross appears again in heaven,
Even before Elijah comes to gather his own,
The good Shepherd goes silently through the lands.
Now and then he gathers from the depths of the abyss
A little lamb, shelters it at his heart.
And then others always follow him.
But there above the throne of grace
The Mother ceaselessly pleads for her people.
She seeks souls to help her pray.
Then only when Israel has found the Lord,
Only then when he has received his own,
Will he come in manifest glory.
And we must pray for this second coming.

Scripture

Micah 5:2–5

But you, O Bethlehem of Ephrathah,
who are one of the little clans of Judah,
from you shall come forth for me
one who is to rule in Israel,
whose origin is from of old,
from ancient days.
Therefore he shall give them up until the time
when she who is in labor has brought forth;
then the rest of his kindred shall return
to the people of Israel.
And he shall stand and feed his flock in the strength of the Lord,
in the majesty of the name of the Lord his God.
And they shall live secure, for now he shall be great
to the ends of the earth;
and he shall be the one of peace.

Reflection

Bishop Barron

Catholicism

The Cathedral of Chartres is one of the most sumptuous and beautiful enclosed spaces in the world. Like almost all of the other Gothic cathedrals that sprang up in France in the twelfth and thirteenth centuries, Chartres is dedicated to *Notre Dame* (Our Lady).

All around this building dedicated to the Blessed Mother are depictions of figures from the Old Testament—Adam, Job, David, Moses, Aaron—and this is only appropriate, for Mary, the Mother of God, is the fulfillment of Zion. She recapitulates all of the great figures of the holy people whom God had prepared, in the course of many centuries, to receive his Word and make it flesh. She is, accordingly, the daughter of Abraham, the first one to listen to God in faith; she is like Sarah, Hannah, and the mother of Samson, since she gave birth while trusting in God against all expectations; she is the true Ark of the Covenant and the true Temple, for she bore the divine presence in the most intimate way possible; she is like the authors of the Psalms and the book of Wisdom and Proverbs, for she becomes the very seat of Wisdom. And she is like Isaiah, Jeremiah, and Ezekiel—the prophets who longed for the coming of the Messiah.

St. Irenaeus says that throughout the history of salvation God was, as it were, trying on humanity, gradually suiting divinity and humanity to each other—in a word, preparing for the Incarnation. All of that preparation was a prelude to the Israelite girl, full of grace, who would say yes to the invitation to be the Mother of God.

Catechism

64

Through the prophets, God forms his people in the hope of salvation, in the expectation of a new and everlasting Covenant intended for all, to be written on their hearts (see Isa. 2:2–4; Jer. 31:31–34; Heb. 10:16). The prophets proclaim a radical redemption of the People of God, purification from all their infidelities, a salvation which will include all the nations (see Ezek. 36; Isa. 49:5–6, 53:11). Above all, the poor and humble of the Lord will bear this hope. Such holy women as Sarah, Rebecca, Rachel, Miriam, Deborah, Hannah, Judith, and Esther kept alive the hope of Israel's salvation. The purest figure among them is Mary (see Zeph. 2:3; Luke 1:38).

Reflection

Hans Urs von Balthasar

Light of the Word

Seen from the perspective of salvation history, Micah's astonishing prophecy . . . glimpses more of the future than the prophet could have possibly realized. In the time of tribulation following the destruction of Samaria, he returns to the origins of David, who had come from Bethlehem and the tribe of Ephraim in the distant past. According to the prophecy, after the tribulation of the exile has passed, the Shepherd of Israel will come from that place to establish a worldwide peaceable kingdom. Isaiah had spoken of the young woman who would bear the "God-with-us"; here the mother of the Messiah is simply called the "birth-giver." The prophet reaches back to David, but the "distant past of Jesus" is eternity, and his eschatological peaceable kingdom will far surpass Israel's expectations. Perhaps the fulfillment in Mary and her son reaches back to the Old Covenant only in order to tower high above it.

Prayer

St. Methodius of Olympus

Oration Concerning Simeon and Anna

Tremendous, truly, is the mystery connected with you, O virgin mother, spiritual throne, glorified and made worthy of God. You have brought forth, before the eyes of those in heaven and earth, a preeminent wonder. And it is a proof of this, and an irrefragable argument, that at the novelty of thy supernatural child-bearing, the angels sang on earth, "Glory to God in the highest heaven, and on earth peace among those whom he favors," by their threefold song bringing in a threefold holiness. Blessed art you among the generations of women, O most blessed of God, for by you the earth has been filled with that divine glory of God; as in the Psalms it is sung: "Blessed be his glorious name forever; may his glory fill the whole earth. Amen and Amen."

For if to the ark, which was the image and type of your sanctity, such honor was paid to God that to no one but the priestly order was the access to it open, or ingress allowed to behold it, the veil separating it off, and keeping the vestibule as that of a queen—what sort of veneration is due to you from us who are of creation the least, to you who are indeed a Queen; to you, the living Ark of God, the Lawgiver; to you, the heaven that contains him who can be contained of none? For since you, O holy virgin, have dawned as a bright day upon the world, and have brought forth the Sun of Righteousness, that hateful horror of darkness has been chased away; the power of the tyrant has been broken, death has been destroyed, hell swallowed up, and all enmity dissolved before the face of peace.

Amen.

The Sacred Scriptures of both the Old and the New Testament, as well as ancient Tradition, show the role of the Mother of the Savior in the economy of salvation in an ever clearer light and draw attention to it.

—*LUMEN GENTIUM*

The Virgin Shall Bear a Son

Poem

Gerard Manley Hopkins

From "The Blessed Virgin compared to the Air we Breathe"

Wild air, world-mothering air,
Nestling me everywhere,
That each eyelash or hair
Girdles; goes home betwixt
The fleeciest, frailest-flixed
Snowflake; that's fairly mixed
With, riddles, and is rife
In every least thing's life;
This needful, never spent,
And nursing element;
My more than meat and drink,
My meal at every wink;
This air, which, by life's law,
My lung must draw and draw
Now but to breathe its praise,
Minds me in many ways
Of her who not only
Gave God's infinity

Dwindled to infancy
Welcome in womb and breast,
Birth, milk, and all the rest
But mothers each new grace
That does now reach our race—
Mary Immaculate,
Merely a woman, yet
Whose presence, power is
Great as no goddess's
Was deemèd, dreamèd; who
This one work has to do—
Let all God's glory through,
God's glory which would go
Through her and from her flow
Off, and no way but so. . . .
 Be thou then, thou dear
Mother, my atmosphere;
My happier world, wherein
To wend and meet no sin;
Above me, round me lie
Fronting my froward eye
With sweet and scarless sky;
Stir in my ears, speak there
Of God's love, O live air,
Of patience, penance, prayer:
World-mothering air, air wild,

Wound with thee, in thee isled,
Fold home, fast fold thy child.

Scripture

Isaiah 7:13–14

Then Isaiah said: "Hear then, O house of David! Is it too little for you to weary mortals, that you weary my God also? Therefore the Lord himself will give you a sign. Look, the young woman[1] is with child and shall bear a son, and shall name him Immanuel."

Reflection

Bishop Barron

Light from Light

Many skeptics across the ages have put the doctrine of the Virgin Birth of Jesus forward as an indisputable sign that the Church is retrograde, stuck in a prescientific, superstitious mindset. Is not the birth of Jesus from a virgin, they wonder, just another iteration of a mythic trope found in cultures around the world?

First, as Hans Urs von Balthasar has argued, the story of the birth of Jesus from a virgin and those similar narratives from mythic traditions are only superficially similar. The more intently one studies the Gospel stories, the more unique and

1. Greek: "the virgin."

distinctive they appear. But the most striking difference is that the myths give themselves away by their very genre: they are, quite obviously, symbolic literature, intended to indicate natural processes or general truths about the rhythms of the seasons. But the Gospel narratives concerning the birth of Jesus are placed very purposely within a recognizable historical and geographical context, grounding them in fact: "A decree went out from Emperor Augustus . . . while Quirinius was governor of Syria" (Luke 2:1–2). And they are a propaedeutic to what is assuredly the biography of a real, historical figure, clearly unlike the narratives concerning Horus or Mars.

But is this teaching, the critics insist, not simply repugnant to reason, even if we grant that it differs from similar accounts? That skeptical claim is grounded in the meta-assertion that the miraculous, strictly speaking, is impossible. However, once we affirm the existence of God, which can be done on rational grounds, this dismissal of the miraculous appears more or less arbitrary. To be sure, miracles are rare, for if they were not, we would not "wonder" at them, which is the state of mind implied in the word *mirari*. But what would prevent the creative source of all finite existence, who continually makes the world from nothing and sustains it from falling back into nonbeing, from producing a state of affairs outside of the normal course? What would be irrational about saying that God, on rare occasion and for his very particular purposes, might suspend or circumvent the natural regularities that he himself established? If God can bring something from nothing, he can surely cause a virgin to become pregnant.

Mary the Virgin also carries an extraordinarily powerful symbolic value for those with eyes to see. On the façade of Notre Dame Cathedral in Paris, there is a statue of Mary the Mother of God, and over her head is a depiction of the ark of the covenant, the holiest artifact in ancient Israel, the ceremonial container for the Ten Commandments and the rod of Aaron. The association is far from accidental, for Mary was seen as the fulfillment *par excellence* of the ark, since she herself bore the presence of God within her womb.

And if we allow our symbolic and associative imaginations even wider play, we can see Mary, as the Church Fathers did, as evocative of the holy people Israel itself, who bore, over long centuries and through much suffering, the word of Yahweh. It is from Mary's womb, and indeed from the womb of Israel, that the Messiah is born.

Catechism

496–498, 506–507

From the first formulations of her faith, the Church has confessed that Jesus was conceived solely by the power of the Holy Spirit in the womb of the Virgin Mary, affirming also the corporeal aspect of this event: Jesus was conceived "by the Holy

Spirit without human seed."[2] The Fathers see in the virginal conception the sign that it truly was the Son of God who came in a humanity like our own. Thus St. Ignatius of Antioch at the beginning of the second century says:

> You are firmly convinced about our Lord, who is truly of the race of David according to the flesh, Son of God according to the will and power of God, truly born of a virgin, . . . he was truly nailed to a tree for us in his flesh under Pontius Pilate . . . he truly suffered, as he is also truly risen.[3]

The gospel accounts understand the virginal conception of Jesus as a divine work that surpasses all human understanding and possibility (see Matt. 1:18-25; Luke 1:26–38): "That which is conceived in her is of the Holy Spirit," said the angel to Joseph about Mary his fiancée (Matt. 1:20). The Church sees here the fulfillment of the divine promise given through the prophet Isaiah: "Behold, a virgin shall conceive and bear a son" (Isa. 7:14; see Matt. 1:23).

People are sometimes troubled by the silence of St. Mark's Gospel and the New Testament Epistles about Jesus' virginal conception. Some might wonder if we were merely dealing with legends or theological constructs not claiming to be history. To

---

2. Council of the Lateran (649): Denzinger-Schönmetzer 503; see DS 10–64.

3. St. Ignatius of Antioch, *Ad Smyrn.* 1–2: The Apostolic Fathers, ed. J.B. Lightfoot (London: Macmillan, 1889) II/2, 289–293; SCh 10, 154–156; see Rom. 1:3; John 1:13.

this we must respond: Faith in the virginal conception of Jesus met with the lively opposition, mockery, or incomprehension of non-believers, Jews and pagans alike;[4] so it could hardly have been motivated by pagan mythology or by some adaptation to the ideas of the age. The meaning of this event is accessible only to faith, which understands in it the "connection of these mysteries with one another"[5] in the totality of Christ's mysteries, from his Incarnation to his Passover. St. Ignatius of Antioch already bears witness to this connection: "Mary's virginity and giving birth, and even the Lord's death escaped the notice of the prince of this world: these three mysteries worthy of proclamation were accomplished in God's silence."[6] . . .

Mary is a virgin because her virginity is *the sign of her faith* "unadulterated by any doubt," and of her undivided gift of herself to God's will.[7] It is her faith that enables her to become the mother of the Savior: "Mary is more blessed because she embraces faith in Christ than because she conceives the flesh of Christ."[8]

At once virgin and mother, Mary is the symbol and the most perfect realization of the Church: "the Church indeed . . . by receiving the word of God in faith becomes herself a mother.

---

4. See St. Justin, *Dial.*, 99, 7: Patrologia Graeca 6, 708–709; Origen, *Contra Celsum* 1, 32, 69: PG 11, 720–721; et al.
5. *Dei Filius* 4: DS 3016.
6. St. Ignatius of Antioch, *Ad Eph.* 19, 1: The Apostolic Fathers II/2, 76–80; SCh 10, 88; see 1 Cor. 2:8.
7. *Lumen Gentium* 63; see 1 Cor. 7:34–35.
8. St. Augustine, *De virg.*, 3: Patrologia Latina 40, 398.

By preaching and Baptism she brings forth sons, who are conceived by the Holy Spirit and born of God, to a new and immortal life. She herself is a virgin, who keeps in its entirety and purity the faith she pledged to her spouse."[9]

Reflection

St. Thomas Aquinas
Summa theologiae

It is fitting for four reasons that Christ should be born of a virgin. First, in order to maintain the dignity of the Father who sent him. For since Christ is the true and natural Son of God, it was not fitting that he should have another father than God: lest the dignity belonging to God be transferred to another.

Secondly, this was befitting to a property of the Son himself, who is sent. For he is the Word of God: and the word is conceived without any interior corruption: indeed, interior corruption is incompatible with perfect conception of the word. Since therefore flesh was so assumed by the Word of God, as to be the flesh of the Word of God, it was fitting that it also should be conceived without corruption of the mother.

Thirdly, this was befitting to the dignity of Christ's humanity in which there could be no sin, since by it the sin of the world was taken away, according to John 1:29: "Here is the Lamb of God" (i.e., the Lamb without stain) "who takes away the sin of the world." Now it was not possible in a nature

9. *LG* 64; see *LG* 63.

already corrupt, for flesh to be born from sexual intercourse without incurring the infection of original sin. Whence Augustine says (*De Nup. et Concup.* i): "In that union," viz. the marriage of Mary and Joseph, "the nuptial intercourse alone was lacking: because in sinful flesh this could not be without fleshly concupiscence which arises from sin, and without which he wished to be conceived, who was to be without sin."

Fourthly, on account of the very end of Incarnation of Christ, which was that men might be born again as sons of God, "not of . . . the will of the flesh or of the will of man, but of God" (John 1:13), i.e., of the power of God, of which fact the very conception of Christ was to appear as an exemplar. Whence Augustine says (*De Sanct. Virg.*): "It behooved that our Head, by a notable miracle, should be born, after the flesh, of a virgin, that he might thereby signify that his members would be born, after the Spirit, of a virgin Church."

Prayer

St. Thomas Aquinas (attributed)

Virgin full of goodness,
Mother of mercy,
I entrust to you my body and my soul,
my thoughts and my actions,
my life and my death.

My Queen,
come to my aid
and deliver me from the snares of the devil.
Obtain for me the grace of loving
my Lord Jesus Christ, your son,
with a true and perfect love,
and after him, O Mary,
of loving you with all my heart
and above all things.
Amen.

Since an unlooked-for salvation was to be provided for men through the help of God, so also was the unlooked-for birth from a virgin accomplished—God giving this sign, but man not working it out.

—ST. IRENAEUS

The Immaculate Conception

Poem

Paul Claudel

From "The Virgin at Noon"

It is noon. The church is open. I must go in.
Mother of our Lord, I have not come to pray.

I have nothing to give and nothing to ask.
I am here, my Lady, only to look at you.

To look at you, to cry for joy, to know
That I am your son and you are there.

Only for one moment when everything stops.
Noon!
To be with you, Mary, in this place where you are.

To say nothing, to look at your face,
To let my heart sing in its own language,

To say nothing, but simply to sing because my heart is too full,
Like the blackbird which repeats its idea in that species of swift couplets.

Because you are beautiful, because you are pure,
Woman at last restored in Grace,

Creature in her first honor and her final glory,
As she came from God in the morning of her original splendor.

Intact ineffably because you are the Mother of Our Lord,
Who is the truth in your arms, and the only hope and the one fruit.

Because you are woman, the Eden of the ancient forgotten tenderness,
Whose eyes look suddenly into the heart and cause the pent-up tears to flow . . .

Because it is noon, because we are at this moment of today,

Because you are there for always, simply because you are Mary, simply because you exist,
Mother of Our Lord, we give thanks to you!

Scripture

Luke 1:26–45

In the sixth month the angel Gabriel was sent by God to a town in Galilee called Nazareth, to a virgin engaged to a man whose name was Joseph, of the house of David. The virgin's name was Mary. And he came to her and said, "Greetings, favored one! The Lord is with you." But she was much perplexed by his words and pondered what sort of greeting this might be. The angel said to her, "Do not be afraid, Mary, for you have found favor with God. And now, you will conceive in your womb and bear a son, and you will name him Jesus. He will be great, and will be called the Son of the Most High, and the Lord God will give to him the throne of his ancestor David. He will reign over the house of Jacob forever, and of his kingdom there will be no end." Mary said to the angel, "How can this be, since I am a virgin?" The angel said to her, "The Holy Spirit will come upon you, and the power of the Most High will overshadow you; therefore the child to be born will be holy; he will be called Son of God. And now, your relative Elizabeth in her old age has also conceived a son; and this is the sixth month for her who was said to be barren. For nothing will be impossible with God." Then Mary said, "Here am I, the servant of the Lord; let it be with me according to your word." Then the angel departed from her.

In those days Mary set out and went with haste to a

Judean town in the hill country, where she entered the house of Zechariah and greeted Elizabeth. When Elizabeth heard Mary's greeting, the child leaped in her womb. And Elizabeth was filled with the Holy Spirit and exclaimed with a loud cry, "Blessed are you among women, and blessed is the fruit of your womb. And why has this happened to me, that the mother of my Lord comes to me? For as soon as I heard the sound of your greeting, the child in my womb leaped for joy. And blessed is she who believed that there would be a fulfillment of what was spoken to her by the Lord."

Reflection

Bishop Barron
Catholicism

The dogma of the Immaculate Conception was formally declared only recently, but its provenance is quite ancient. Indications of the doctrine can be traced to the New Testament in the angel's greeting to Mary: "Greetings, favored one! The Lord is with you" (Luke 1:28). Perhaps what we notice first about this and other Marian dogmas is how physical, even disturbingly so, they are—how they compel us to see God's activity in the functions and destiny of the lowly human body. The English Catholic novelist David Lodge has observed that upon hearing of this and similar doctrines, his Protestant school friends were ashamed to tell their parents about them!

In 1854, Pope Pius IX declared the dogma of the Immaculate Conception of Mary—which is to say, the truth that Mary, through a special grace, was preserved free from original sin from the first moment of her conception. Were this not the case, the angel would not have referred to her at the Annunciation as *Kecharitomene* (full of grace). Two questions naturally present themselves when this doctrine is proposed: Why would God do such a thing? And wouldn't this imply that Mary does not need to be redeemed? The traditional answer to the first question is that God wanted to prepare a worthy vessel for the reception of his Word. Just as the holy of holies in the temple was kept pure and inviolate, so the definitive Temple, the true Ark of the Covenant, which is Mary herself, should all the more be untrammeled. In this context, the stories concerning the young Mary's close association with the temple in Jerusalem (found in the *Protoevangelium of James*, a second-century text) are, if not necessarily historically accurate, nevertheless theologically suggestive.

Even some of the finest minds in the Church have found the second question difficult to answer. Though liturgies celebrating the Immaculate Conception date from the seventh century, theologians as weighty as Alexander of Hales, St. Bonaventure, and St. Thomas Aquinas himself couldn't find a sufficient justification for the teaching. It appeared to them that to declare Mary free of original sin from the moment of her conception would preclude the universality of Christ's redemptive act, which took place many years after Mary was conceived. It was Blessed John Duns Scotus who, in the early fourteenth century, showed a way forward. He argued that Mary is indeed, like the rest of the human race, redeemed by the grace of her son, but since that grace exists, properly speaking, outside of time, it can be applied in a way that transcends the ordinary rhythms of time. Therefore, Mary was preemptively delivered by Christ's grace from original sin. With typical scholastic laconicism, Duns Scotus said with regard to God's effecting of this deliverance: "Potuit, decuit, ergo fecit" (He could do it; it was fitting that he do it; therefore, he did it).

Catechism

490–493

To become the mother of the Savior, Mary "was enriched by God with gifts appropriate to such a role."[1] The angel Gabriel at the moment of the Annunciation salutes her as "full of grace" (Luke 1:28). In fact, in order for Mary to be able to give the free assent of her faith to the announcement of her vocation, it was necessary that she be wholly borne by God's grace.

Through the centuries the Church has become ever more aware that Mary, "full of grace" through God (Luke 1:28), was redeemed from the moment of her conception. That is what the

1. *Lumen Gentium* 56.

dogma of the Immaculate Conception confesses, as Pope Pius IX proclaimed in 1854:

> The most Blessed Virgin Mary was, from the first moment of her conception, by a singular grace and privilege of almighty God and by virtue of the merits of Jesus Christ, Savior of the human race, preserved immune from all stain of original sin.[2]

The "splendor of an entirely unique holiness" by which Mary is "enriched from the first instant of her conception" comes wholly from Christ: she is "redeemed, in a more exalted fashion, by reason of the merits of her Son."[3] The Father blessed Mary more than any other created person "in Christ with every spiritual blessing in the heavenly places" and chose her "in Christ before the foundation of the world, to be holy and blameless before him in love" (see Eph. 1:3–4).

The Fathers of the Eastern tradition call the Mother of God "the All-Holy" (*Panagia*) and celebrate her as "free from any stain of sin, as though fashioned by the Holy Spirit and formed as a new creature."[4] By the grace of God Mary remained free of every personal sin her whole life long.

---

2. Pius IX, *Ineffabilis Deus*, 1854: Denzinger-Schönmetzer 2803.
3. *LG* 53, 56.
4. *LG* 56.

Reflection

St. John Henry Newman

Meditations on the Litany of Loretto, for the Month of May

Mary is the *Virgo Praedicanda*, that is, the Virgin who is to be proclaimed, to be heralded; literally, to be *preached*.

We are accustomed to preach abroad that which is wonderful, strange, rare, novel, important. Thus, when our Lord was coming, St. John the Baptist *preached* him; then, the Apostles went into the wide world, and *preached* Christ. What is the highest, the rarest, the choicest prerogative of Mary? It is that she was without sin. When a woman in the crowd cried out to our Lord, "Blessed is the womb that bore you!" he answered, "Blessed rather are those who hear the word of God and obey it!" (Luke 11:27–28). Those words were fulfilled in Mary. She was filled with grace *in order* to be the Mother of God. But it was a higher gift than her maternity to be thus sanctified and thus pure. Our Lord indeed would not have become her son unless he had first sanctified her; but still, the greater blessedness was to have that perfect sanctification.

This then is why she is the *Virgo Praedicanda*; she is deserving to be preached abroad because she never committed any sin, even the least; because sin had no part in her; because, through the fullness of God's grace, she never thought a thought, or spoke a word, or did an action, which was displeasing, which was not most pleasing, to Almighty God; because in her was displayed the greatest triumph over the enemy of souls. Wherefore, when all seemed lost, in order to show what he could do for us all by dying for us; in order to show what human nature, his work, was capable of becoming; to show how utterly he could bring to naught the utmost efforts, the most concentrated malice of the foe, and reverse all the consequences of the fall, our Lord began, even before his coming, to do his most wonderful act of redemption, in the person of her who was to be his Mother. By the merit of that blood which was to be shed, he interposed to hinder her incurring the sin of Adam, before he had made on the cross atonement for it. And therefore it is that we *preach* her who is the subject of this wonderful grace.

Prayer

St. Pio of Pietrelcina (Padre Pio)

Meditation Prayer on Mary Immaculate

My most pure Mother, my soul so poor, all stained with wretchedness and sin, cries out to your maternal heart. In your goodness deign, I beseech you, to pour out on me at least a little of the grace that flowed into you with such infinite profusion from the Heart of God. Strengthened and supported by this grace, may I succeed in better loving and serving Almighty God who filled your heart completely, and who created the temple of your body from the moment of your Immaculate Conception. . . .

Oh my Mother, how ashamed I feel in your presence, weighted down as I am with faults! You are most pure and immaculate from the moment of your conception, indeed from the moment in eternity when you were conceived in the mind of God.

Have pity on me! May one compassionate look of yours revive me, purify me, and lift me up to God, raising me from the filth of this world that I may go to him who created me, who regenerated me in Holy Baptism, giving me back my white stole of innocence that original sin had so defiled. Dear Mother, make me love him! Pour into my heart that love that burned in yours for him. Even though I be clothed in misery, I revere the mystery of your Immaculate Conception, and I ardently wish that through it you may purify my heart so that I may love your God and my God. Cleanse my mind that it may reach up to him and contemplate him and adore him in spirit and in truth. Purify my body that I too may be a tabernacle for him and be less unworthy of possessing him when he deigns to come to me in Holy Communion.

Amen.

Mary, the New Woman, stands at the side of Christ, the New Man, within whose mystery the mystery of man alone finds true light; she is given to it as a pledge and guarantee that God's plan in Christ for the salvation of the whole man has already achieved realization in a creature: in her.

—POPE ST. PAUL VI

Sing, O Daughter Zion

Poem

Gerard Manley Hopkins
"The May Magnificat"

May is Mary's month, and I
Muse at that and wonder why:
  Her feasts follow reason,
  Dated due to season—

Candlemas, Lady Day;
But the Lady Month, May,
  Why fasten that upon her,
  With a feasting in her honour?

Is it only its being brighter
Than the most are must delight her?
  Is it opportunest
  And flowers finds soonest?

Ask of her, the mighty mother:
Her reply puts this other
  Question: What is Spring?—
  Growth in every thing—

Flesh and fleece, fur and feather,
Grass and green world all together;
  Star-eyed strawberry-breasted
  Throstle above her nested

Cluster of bugle blue eggs thin
Forms and warms the life within;
  And bird and blossom swell
  In sod or sheath or shell.

All things rising, all things sizing
Mary sees, sympathising
  With that world of good,
  Nature's motherhood.

Their magnifying of each its kind
With delight calls to mind
  How she did in her stored
  Magnify the Lord.

Well but there was more than this:
Spring's universal bliss
  Much, had much to say
  To offering Mary May.

When drop-of-blood-and-foam-dapple
Bloom lights the orchard-apple
  And thicket and thorp are merry
  With silver-surfèd cherry

And azuring-over greybell makes
Wood banks and brakes wash wet like lakes
  And magic cuckoocall
  Caps, clears, and clinches all—

This ecstacy all through mothering earth
Tells Mary her mirth till Christ's birth
  To remember and exultation
  In God who was her salvation.

Scripture

Zephaniah 3:14–20

Sing aloud, O daughter Zion;
  shout, O Israel!
Rejoice and exult with all your heart,
  O daughter Jerusalem!
The Lord has taken away the judgments against you,
  he has turned away your enemies.

The king of Israel, the Lord, is in your midst;
   you shall fear disaster no more.
On that day it shall be said to Jerusalem:
   Do not fear, O Zion;
   do not let your hands grow weak.
The Lord, your God, is in your midst,
   a warrior who gives victory;
he will rejoice over you with gladness,
   he will renew you in his love;
he will exult over you with loud singing
   as on a day of festival.
I will remove disaster from you,
   so that you will not bear reproach for it.
I will deal with all your oppressors
   at that time.
And I will save the lame
   and gather the outcast,
and I will change their shame into praise
   and renown in all the earth.
At that time I will bring you home,
   at the time when I gather you;
for I will make you renowned and praised
   among all the peoples of the earth,
when I restore your fortunes
   before your eyes, says the Lord.

Luke 1:46–55

And Mary said,
"My soul magnifies the Lord,
  and my spirit rejoices in God my Savior,
for he has looked with favor on the lowliness of his servant.
  Surely, from now on all generations will call me blessed;
for the Mighty One has done great things for me,
  and holy is his name.
His mercy is for those who fear him
  from generation to generation.
He has shown strength with his arm;
  he has scattered the proud in the thoughts of their hearts.
He has brought down the powerful from their thrones,
  and lifted up the lowly;
he has filled the hungry with good things,
  and sent the rich away empty.
He has helped his servant Israel,
  in remembrance of his mercy,
according to the promise he made to our ancestors,
  to Abraham and to his descendants forever."

Reflection

Bishop Barron

Catholicism

In the first chapter of the Gospel of Luke, we find Mary's great hymn of praise to Yahweh. It commences with the simple declaration, "My soul magnifies the Lord, and my spirit rejoices in God my Savior" (Luke 1:46–47). Mary announces here that her whole being is ordered to the glorification of God. Her ego wants nothing for itself; it wants only to be an occasion for giving honor to God. But since God needs nothing, whatever glory Mary gives to him returns to her benefit so that she is magnified in the very act of magnifying him. In giving herself away fully to God, Mary becomes a superabundant source of life; indeed, she becomes pregnant with God. This odd and wonderful rhythm of magnifying and being magnified is the key to understanding everything about Mary, from her divine motherhood, to her Assumption and her Immaculate Conception, to her mission in the life of the Church.

The great nineteenth-century Jesuit poet Gerard Manley Hopkins caught this in his ballad "The May Magnificat." He wonders aloud in the first few stanzas why May should be a month dedicated to Mary, and he provides Mary's own answer:

> Ask of her, the mighty mother:
> Her reply puts this other

Question: What is Spring?—
Growth in every thing—

Then, with typical verbal dexterity and spiritual enthusiasm, Hopkins delineates the modes of growth in springtime, and he imagines Mary the Mother of God surveying all of this life with limitless pleasure:

All things rising, all things sizing
Mary sees, sympathising
  With that world of good,
  Nature's motherhood.

Mary's utter willingness to magnify the Lord made of her a matrix of life. The spring itself, in all of its wild fecundity, is but a hint at the vitality that she unleashes.

Catechism

2617–2619

Mary's prayer is revealed to us at the dawning of the fullness of time. Before the Incarnation of the Son of God, and before the outpouring of the Holy Spirit, her prayer cooperates in a unique way with the Father's plan of loving kindness: at the Annunciation, for Christ's conception; at Pentecost, for the formation of the Church, his Body (see Luke 1:38; Acts 1:14).

In the faith of his humble handmaid, the Gift of God found the acceptance he had awaited from the beginning of time. She whom the Almighty made "full of grace" responds by offering her whole being: "Behold I am the handmaid of the Lord; let it be [done] to me according to your word." "*Fiat*": this is Christian prayer: to be wholly God's, because he is wholly ours.

The Gospel reveals to us how Mary prays and intercedes in faith. At Cana (see John 2:1–12), the mother of Jesus asks her son for the needs of a wedding feast; this is the sign of another feast—that of the wedding of the Lamb where he gives his body and blood at the request of the Church, his Bride. It is at the hour of the New Covenant, at the foot of the cross (see John 19:25–27), that Mary is heard as the Woman, the new Eve, the true "Mother of all the living."

That is why the Canticle of Mary (see Luke 1:46–55), the *Magnificat* (Latin) or *Megalynei* (Byzantine), is the song both of the Mother of God and of the Church; the song of the Daughter of Zion and of the new People of God; the song of thanksgiving for the fullness of graces poured out in the economy of salvation and the song of the "poor" whose hope is met by the fulfillment of the promises made to our ancestors, "to Abraham and to his posterity for ever."

Reflection

St. Louis de Montfort

A Treatise on the True Devotion to the Blessed Virgin

She embellishes our works, in adorning them with her own merits and virtues. It is as if a peasant, wishing to gain the friendship and benevolence of the king, went to the queen, and presented her with a fruit, which was his whole revenue, in order that she might present it to the king. The queen, having accepted the poor little offering from the peasant, would place the fruit on a large and beautiful dish of gold, and so, on the peasant's behalf, would present it to the king. Then the fruit, however unworthy in itself to be a king's present, would become worthy of his majesty, because of the dish of gold on which it rested and the person who presented it.

She presents these good works to Jesus Christ; for she keeps nothing of what is given for herself, as if she was our last end. She refers it all faithfully to Jesus. If we give to her, we give necessarily to Jesus; if we praise her or glorify her, we at once praise and glorify Jesus. As of old, when St. Elizabeth praised her, so now, when we praise and bless her, she sings herself, *Magnificat anima mea Dominum* (My soul magnifies the Lord).

Prayer

St. Catherine of Siena
"Prayer 18"

O Mary!
Mary!
Temple of the Trinity!
O Mary, bearer of the fire!
Mary, minister of mercy!
Mary, seedbed of the fruit! . . .

O Mary, peaceful sea!
Mary, giver of peace!
Mary, fertile soil!
You, Mary, are the new-sprung plant
from whom we have the fragrant blossom,
the Word, God's only-begotten Son,
for in you, fertile soil,
was this Word sown.
You are the soil
and you are the plant.
O Mary, chariot of fire,
you bore the fire
hidden and veiled
under the ashes of your humanness.

O Mary, vessel of humility!
In you the light of true knowledge
thrives and burns.
By this light
you rose above yourself,
and so you were pleasing to the eternal Father,
and he seized you and drew you to himself,
loving you with a special love. . . .

O Mary,
may you be proclaimed blessed among all women
for endless ages,
for today you have shared with us
your flour.
Today the Godhead
is joined and kneaded into one dough
with our humanity—
so securely
that this union could never be broken,
either by death
or by our thanklessness. . . .
It will never be dissolved,
any more than it has been broken up to now.
Amen.

Transcending all problems,
Marian devotion is the rapture
of joy over the true, indestructible
Israel; it is a blissful entering
into the joy of the Magnificat
and thereby it is the praise of
him to whom the daughter Zion
owes her whole self and whom
she bears, the true, incorruptible,
indestructible Ark of the
Covenant.

—JOSEPH RATZINGER
(POPE BENEDICT XVI)

Hymn

Salve Regina

(Sung from Pentecost Sunday to the First Sunday of Advent)

Latin

Salve, Regina, mater misericordiae;
vita, dulcedo et spes nostra, salve.
Ad te clamamus, exsules filii Evae.
Ad te suspiramus, gementes et flentes
in hac lacrimarum valle.

Eia ergo, advocata nostra,
illos tuos misericordes oculos
ad nos converte.
Et Iesum, benedictum fructum ventris tui,
nobis post hoc exsilium ostende.
O clemens, o pia, o dulcis Virgo Maria.

English

Hail, holy Queen, mother of mercy,
our life, our sweetness, and our hope.
To thee do we cry, poor banished children of Eve;
to thee do we send up our sighs,
mourning and weeping in this valley of tears.

Turn, then, most gracious advocate,
thine eyes of mercy toward us;
and after this, our exile,
show unto us the blessed fruit of thy womb, Jesus.
O clement, O loving, O sweet Virgin Mary.

II.
Mother *of* Jesus

✷ His Face

Sally Read

His body is swaddled head to foot,
but his face is a window: one small pool of light.
This nakedness, that even Adam would not cover,
is a tender dish of listening, hunger
in the nuzzling nose and petal mouth, a sense
of all in the here and now—and dizzy distance,
like that one star announcing the expanse
of night. Lady, see the depths of his dark eyes.
This locked gaze is what keeps God and man
together. It is true prayer: he holding fast
to your face like a constellated sky; you tumbling
softly into him with no lights but those eyes.

The Spouse of the Spirit

Poem

Condé Benoist Pallen

From "Maria Immaculata"

The great archangel veils his face
Before her: "Hail, full of grace!"
And Heaven is clasped of earth;
While all the wheeling spheres with all their choirs
Around her wheel seraphic fires.
Eden rises to its second birth;
Again the prime estate
Of man is renovate,
And all the elder worth renewed in her immaculate;
Virgin and spouse of Him
Who breathes the virtue of the Seraphim,
Virgin and mother of the Eternal Son,
Daughter, Virgin, Spouse in one!
The spotless mate of spotless Dove,
The one great miracle of God's love,
From all eternity the chosen bride,
Save only her none, none
Exempt from sin's dominion;

Save only her of Adam's race
Or heavenly line, none full of grace;
On her alone, on her alone
The torrent of His love poured down
The deep abundance of its flood
Into the pure channels of her maidenhood,
The fleckless mirror of her grace
Reflecting all the beauty of His Face.

Scripture

Matthew 1:18–25

Now the birth of Jesus the Messiah took place in this way. When his mother Mary had been engaged to Joseph, but before they lived together, she was found to be with child from the Holy Spirit. Her husband Joseph, being a righteous man and unwilling to expose her to public disgrace, planned to dismiss her quietly. But just when he had resolved to do this, an angel of the Lord appeared to him in a dream and said, "Joseph, son of David, do not be afraid to take Mary as your wife, for the child conceived in her is from the Holy Spirit. She will bear a son, and you are to name him Jesus, for he will save his people from their sins." All this took place to fulfill what had been spoken by the Lord through the prophet:

"Look, the virgin shall conceive and bear a son,
and they shall name him Emmanuel,"

which means, "God is with us." When Joseph awoke from sleep, he did as the angel of the Lord commanded him; he took her as his wife, but had no marital relations with her until she had borne a son; and he named him Jesus.

Reflection

Bishop Barron
Homily

Many mythologies and philosophies of the ancient world held that time is cyclical. Things turn round and round, always returning to the same place, a bit like the revolutions of the planets and stars. This view was reembraced in modernity by the philosopher Friedrich Nietzsche, who spoke of the "eternal return of the same." Today, many people would say instead that time is essentially meaningless: things just come and go without any discernible rhyme or reason or purpose. What we consider good and bad are more or less relative terms, and therefore it's pointless to say that either is carrying the day.

To both of these finally despairing ideas, we have to contrast the biblical notion that history is purposive. It is heading somewhere, under the direction of a guiding Spirit. Relatedly, time is filled with rhymes and echoes and meaningful hints and trajectories. History is not just one thing after another; it is a kind of story or narrative, told by an author.

Consider the seventh chapter of the book of the prophet Isaiah. The Lord is speaking to Ahaz, a young king of Israel in the line of David, who has come to a particularly challenging time in his reign. He invites the king to dream big, to ask for a sign: "Let it be deep as Sheol or high as heaven" (Isa. 7:11). In other words, ask for anything you want. But Ahaz has lost faith in the Lord and is instead relying on earthly powers, and so he demurs: "I will not ask" (Isa. 7:12). Here, he is like many people today, who refuse to believe that God is in charge and who consequently refuse to dream. So God does him one better: "Therefore the Lord himself will give you a sign. Look, the young woman is with child and shall bear a son, and shall name him Immanuel" (Isa. 7:14). We might give up on God, but he never gives up on us. We might think time and history have no purpose, but God keeps showing us that it does.

To grasp the meaning of this sign fully, we have to go back well before the time of Isaiah and Ahaz, to the reign of King David. In 2 Samuel 7, God promises David that he will put a descendent of his on a throne that will last forever. Up and down the centuries, even when things seemed darkest and most hopeless, Israel never quite forgot this promise. It is precisely this promise that is reiterated to Ahaz.

Now flash forward seven hundred years from this period—remembering that history rhymes!—and consider the extraordinary conversation reported in the first chapter of the Gospel of Matthew. In the little town of Nazareth in Galilee, in a simple home, Joseph, a carpenter betrothed to a young girl called Mary, has just received the devastating news that the woman to whom he is engaged is pregnant—evidently by another man.

We can barely begin to sense how crushing this was for him. The woman he loved had betrayed him (he must have thought); the life he had planned had come undone; he would be humiliated in his community, and if the law of Israel were followed to the letter, Mary would be stoned to death. And that's why, hoping against hope, he resolves to divorce Mary quietly.

Joseph was every bit as beleaguered as Ahaz. We can only imagine how difficult it was for him to sleep. Did he ask God for help, for a sign? We don't know—no word of Joseph is ever recorded in the New Testament—but that night, in his dreams, he did receive a sign, and it was something greater than he ever imagined: "An angel of the Lord appeared to him in a dream and said, 'Joseph, son of David, do not be afraid to take Mary as your wife, for the child conceived in her is from the Holy Spirit. She will bear a son, and you are to name him Jesus, for he will save his people from their sins'" (Matt. 1:20–21).

And then St. Matthew reminds us of what the Lord had said to Ahaz seven centuries before! The child to be born to Mary *is* the son promised long ago to David and to Ahaz, the one who would reign on the throne of David forever. He is the long-awaited Messiah, who draws all of history and time together in himself, the magnetic point toward which all things have, from the beginning of time, been tending.

Catechism

484–485

The Annunciation to Mary inaugurates "the fullness of time" (Gal. 4:4), the time of the fulfillment of God's promises and preparations. Mary was invited to conceive him in whom the "whole fullness of deity" would dwell "bodily" (Col. 2:9). The divine response to her question, "How can this be, since I know not man?" was given by the power of the Spirit: "The Holy Spirit will come upon you" (Luke 1:34–35).

The mission of the Holy Spirit is always conjoined and ordered to that of the Son (see John 16:14–15). The Holy Spirit, "the Lord, the giver of Life," is sent to sanctify the womb of the Virgin Mary and divinely fecundate it, causing her to conceive the eternal Son of the Father in a humanity drawn from her own.

Reflection

Pope St. John Paul II
Homily

Mary was the first to benefit from the light which one day her Jesus would promise to the disciples: "The Advocate, the Holy

Spirit, whom the Father will send in my name, will teach you everything, and remind you of all that I have said to you" (John 14:26). The Holy Spirit who makes the Church and believers understand the meaning and the worth of Christ's words was already working in Mary who as mother of the Word Incarnate was the *Sedes Sapientiae*, the Spouse of the Holy Spirit, the bearer and the first mediatrix of the Gospel concerning Jesus' origins.

Even during the successive years in Nazareth, Mary stored in her heart all that regarded the person and destiny of her son and reflected on it silently. Perhaps she could not confide in anyone. Perhaps only at some particular moment was it granted her to grasp the meaning of certain words, of certain glances given by her son. But the Holy Spirit never stopped reminding her in the intimate depths of her soul of the things she saw and experienced. Mary's memory was enlightened by the light which came from above. That light is at the origin of Luke's narrative, which seems to want to help us understand by insisting on the fact that Mary kept these things and meditated on them. Under the influence of the Holy Spirit's action, she was able to discover the higher meaning of the words and the events, through a reflection which she engaged in, in order to "put everything together."

Thus Mary appears to us to be the model of those who, like the good seed (see Matt. 13:23), allow themselves to be led by the Holy Spirit. They accept and keep in their hearts the words of revelation, making every effort to understand them as much as possible in order to penetrate the depths of Christ's mystery.

Prayer

St. Francis of Assisi
Antiphon

Holy Virgin Mary,
among women,
there is no one like you born into the world:

you are the daughter
and the servant of the most high and supreme King
and Father of heaven,
you are the mother of our most holy Lord Jesus Christ,
you are the spouse of the Holy Spirit.

Pray for us
with St. Michael the Archangel
and all the powers of the heavens
and all the saints
to your most holy beloved Son, the Lord and Master.
Amen.

United to the Holy Spirit as his spouse, she—the Immaculate—is one with God in an incomparably more perfect way than can be predicated of any other creature.

—ST. MAXIMILIAN KOLBE

The Mother of God

Poem

St. Ephrem

From *Hymns on the Nativity of Christ in the Flesh*

Mary gained in You, O Lord, the honors of all married women.
She conceived You within her without marriage.
There was milk in her breasts, not after the way of nature.
You made the thirsty land, suddenly, a fountain of milk.

If she carried You, Your mighty look made her burden light.
If she fed You it was because You were hungry;
if she gave You drink it was because You were thirsty;
when she embraced You, You, the coal of mercies,
did willingly keep her bosom safe.

Your Mother is a wonder.
The Lord entered her, and became a servant:
the Word entered her, and became silent within her;
thunder entered her, and His voice was still:
the Shepherd of all entered her; He became a Lamb in her,
and came forth, bleating.

The belly of Your Mother changed the order of things,
O You that orders everything!
The rich went in, He came out poor.
The high One went in, He came out lowly.
Brightness went into her and clothed Himself
and came out a despised form.

The Mighty went in and clad Himself with fear from the belly.
He that gives food to all went in to know hunger.
He that gives drink to all went in to know thirst.
The clother of all came forth from her naked and bare.

"And as the harp waits for its master,
my mouth waits for You. May the tongue of Your Mother
bring what pleases You;
and since I have learnt a new Conception by You,
let my mouth learn in You, O newborn Son,
a new song of praise.

And if hindrances are no hindrances to You
and since difficulties are easy to You
as a womb without marriage conceived You
and a belly without seed brought You forth
it is easy for a little mouth to multiply Your great glory!"

Scripture

Galatians 4:4–7

When the fullness of time had come, God sent his Son, born of a woman, born under the law, in order to redeem those who were under the law, so that we might receive adoption as children. And because you are children, God has sent the Spirit of his Son into our hearts, crying, "Abba! Father!" So you are no longer a slave but a child, and if a child then also an heir, through God.

Reflection

Bishop Barron

Catholicism

In the year 431, a great council of the church met in the cathedral of Ephesus in order to adjudicate a bitter dispute about the identity of Jesus, but the debate became focused on a technical question in regard to Mary—namely, whether she could legitimately be called *Theotokos*, or Mother of God. The council fathers were trying to understand Jesus more accurately, precisely by teasing out the implications of the conversation that took place between the girl of Nazareth and the angel of the Annunciation.

The background for this council meeting at Ephesus is fascinating. We have to begin by returning to that conversation at Caesarea-Philippi, when Jesus asked the disciples, "Who do people say that I am?" (Mark 8:27). That question, especially in light of the Resurrection, haunted the minds of the members of the ancient Church, and the best intellects of the time strove to answer it accurately. Important steps were taken at the Council of Nicaea in 325, when Jesus was declared to be *homoousios* (one in being) with the Father, and at the Council of Constantinople in 381, when that teaching was reiterated. But in the 420s, a controversy arose over the teaching of Nestorius, who was the patriarch of Constantinople and a much-revered theological figure. Influenced by the school of Antioch, which placed a great stress on the humanity of Jesus, Nestorius suggested that in Christ two distinct persons—one divine and one human—come together in a kind of moral union. This meant that Mary, who was responsible only for the human element in Jesus, could be called *Christotokos* (mother of Christ) but not *Theotokos* (mother of God). In fact, Nestorius argued, the use of that latter title would be the height of blasphemy, since it would imply that a mere human being had a sort of primacy over God. Cyril, the bishop of Alexandria and another theological heavyweight, was so outraged by Nestorius' position that he called the bishop of Constantinople a heretic. The Ecumenical Council of Ephesus was summoned in order to resolve this controversy.

After much deliberation during the summer of 431, the council fathers taught that Jesus ought not to be understood as a human person with a particularly intense relationship to the person of God, for that would make him a kind of supreme saint but not the incarnate Son of God. And if he were not himself divine, he would require a savior as much as anyone else. Rather, it was decided that in the unity of his person both divinity and humanity come together. And this meant, they concluded, that Nestorius was wrong to deny Mary the title *Theotokos*, for if Jesus was divine and Mary was the mother of Jesus, then Mary could and should be called the Mother of God. To Nestorius' point about the blasphemous nature of this description, the council fathers said that Mary is not the mother of Jesus' divinity, but the mother of Jesus, who is, in fact, divine. Historians report that when this resolution was publicly declared, the people of Ephesus responded with a joyful torch-lit parade through the streets of the town. Perhaps these ordinary Christians did not fully grasp the theological subtleties of the conciliar definition, but they understood viscerally that the statement glorified the Virgin Mary whom they loved and who had once lived among them—and so they celebrated.

I would like to spend just a bit more time with those Ephesians who celebrated the *Theotokos*, for some have suggested that the cause for their celebration was deep in their cultural DNA. For centuries, Ephesus had been the center for the lively cult of Artemis, the great mother goddess. In fact, the temple to Artemis, which stood just outside the city, was one of the wonders of the ancient world, more magnificent, Herodotus said, than the pyramids of Egypt or the gardens of Babylon.

Statues of Artemis—covered in dozens of breasts, signifying her nurturing motherhood—were produced at Ephesus and distributed all over the Mediterranean world. Therefore, some have insinuated that Mary simply replaced Artemis in the imagination of the common people, as one more iteration of the mother goddess archetype.

Without denying that there might have been confusion in the minds of some on this score, there in fact yawns a huge gulf between a mother goddess and the Mother of God. The fathers of the Council of Ephesus were not declaring the divinity of Mary; they were not turning the humble handmaid of the Lord into a goddess. But in a certain way they were saying that Mary was indeed greater than Artemis, for she had the privilege, through grace, of bringing into the world the God who would save the world. The declaration of Mary as Mother of God is an instance of the general principle that whatever is said about Mary is meant not so much to draw attention to her as to throw light on Christ. To say that Mary is the Mother of God is to insist on the density of the claim that God truly became human, one of us, bone of our bone and flesh of our flesh. As Archbishop Fulton J. Sheen commented, Mary is like the moon, for her light is always the reflection of a higher light.

Catechism

495

Called in the Gospels "the mother of Jesus," Mary is acclaimed by Elizabeth, at the prompting of the Spirit and even before the birth of her son, as "the mother of my Lord" (Luke 1:43; John 2:1, 19:25; see Matt. 13:55). In fact, the One whom she conceived as man by the Holy Spirit, who truly became her Son according to the flesh, was none other than the Father's eternal Son, the second person of the Holy Trinity. Hence the Church confesses that Mary is truly "Mother of God" (*Theotokos*).[1]

Reflection

St. Cyril of Alexandria
Letter

I am amazed if some should question at all whether the Holy Virgin should be called the Mother of God. For if our Lord Jesus Christ is God, how is the Holy Virgin who bore him not the Mother of God? The inspired disciples transmitted this faith to us, even if they have not made mention of the term. So we have been taught to think by the holy Fathers. . . .

She has borne, not a mere man as we are, but rather the Word of God the Father made flesh, and become man. For we, too, were called gods according to grace, but the Son of God is

1. Council of Ephesus (431): Denzinger-Schönmetzer 251.

not God in this way; rather, he is God according to nature and in truth, even though he was made flesh.

But perhaps you will say this, "Tell me, then, is the Virgin the Mother of his divinity?" And in reply to this we say that his living and subsistent Word was begotten admittedly from the very substance of God and from the Father, and that what was without beginning had a beginning in time, always having existed with his begetter, in him and with him coexisting and coplanning, and that upon the completion of the appointed time when he became flesh, that is when he was united to flesh having a rational soul, that Scripture states he was born of a woman according to the flesh also.

Prayer

"Sub Tuum"

Traditional (from the third century)

We fly to your patronage, O holy Mother of God; despise not our petitions in our necessities; but deliver us from all danger, O ever glorious and blessed Virgin. Amen.

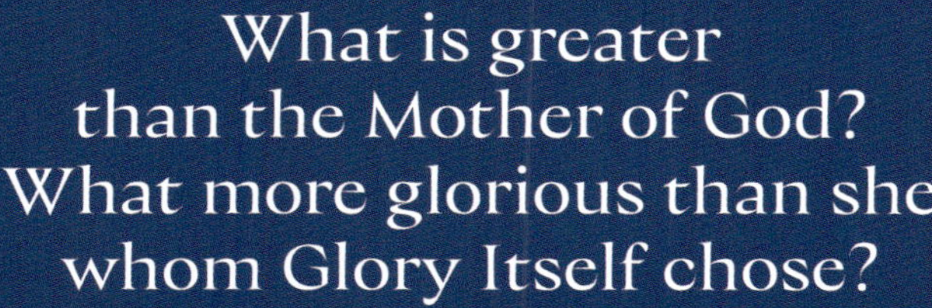
What is greater
than the Mother of God?
What more glorious than she
whom Glory Itself chose?
—ST. AMBROSE

She Pondered in Her Heart

Poem

Caryll Houselander
From "The Reed"

She is a reed,
straight and simple,
growing by a lake
in Nazareth:

a reed that is empty,
until the breath of God
fills it with infinite music:

and the breath of the Spirit of Love
utters the Word of God
through an empty reed.

The Word of God
is infinite music
in a little reed:

it is the sound of a Virgin's heart
beating in the solitude of adoration;
it is a girl's voice
speaking to an angel,
answering for the whole world;

it is the sound of the heart of Christ,
beating within the Virgin's heart;
it is the pulse of God,
timed by the breath of a Child.

Scripture

Luke 2:8–20

In that region there were shepherds living in the fields, keeping watch over their flock by night. Then an angel of the Lord stood before them, and the glory of the Lord shone around them, and they were terrified. But the angel said to them, "Do not be afraid; for see—I am bringing you good news of great joy for all the people: to you is born this day in the city of David a Savior, who is the Messiah, the Lord. This will be a sign for you: you will find a child wrapped in bands of cloth and lying in a manger." And suddenly there was with the angel a multitude of the heavenly host, praising God and saying,

"Glory to God in the highest heaven,
and on earth peace among those whom he favors!"

When the angels had left them and gone into heaven, the shepherds said to one another, "Let us go now to Bethlehem and see this thing that has taken place, which the Lord has made known to us." So they went with haste and found Mary and Joseph, and the child lying in the manger. When they saw this, they made known what had been told them about this child; and all who heard it were amazed at what the shepherds told them. But Mary treasured all these words and pondered them in her heart. The shepherds returned, glorifying and praising God for all they had heard and seen, as it had been told them.

Reflection

Bishop Barron

Redeeming the Time

In the Gospel of Luke, we hear of the visit of the shepherds to Mary and the Christ child in the stable at Bethlehem, and the evangelist tells us that Mary "treasured all these words and pondered them in her heart" (Luke 2:19). Newman said that Mary, precisely in this contemplative, ruminative frame of mind, is the model of all theology.

I'd press it further. She is the real symbol of the Church in its entire function as the custodian of revelation. What is the Sistine Chapel? What is Notre Dame Cathedral? What is the *Divine Comedy* of Dante? What is the *Summa contra Gentiles* of

Thomas Aquinas? What are the sermons of John Chrysostom? What are the teachings of the great ecumenical councils? What is the liturgy in all of its complexity and beauty? These are all means by which the Church stubbornly, century in and century out, treasures the astonishing events of God's self-manifestation. Up and down the ages, the Church ponders what God has done so that the memory of these mighty deeds might never be lost. As such, she performs an indispensable service on behalf of the world—though the world might not have any sense of it. She keeps holding up the light against the darkness.

Catechism

2599

The Son of God who became Son of the Virgin also learned to pray according to his human heart. He learns the formulas of prayer from his mother, who kept in her heart and meditated upon all the "great things" done by the Almighty (see Luke 1:49, 2:19, 2:51).

Reflection

St. John Eudes

The Admirable Heart of Mary

Our Lady cherished the mysteries and marvels of her son's life, first of all, in her material and corporeal heart, the principle of life, the seat of love and of the other physical emotions. All the movements, every beat of this virginal heart, the material functions that it accomplished and the emotions that swayed it, existed solely for Jesus and for the things that concerned him. Her love was spent in loving him, her hatred in hating all that is contrary to him, her joy in rejoicing in his glory and his grandeurs, her sorrow and compassion in bewailing his trials and sufferings. The same may be said of every emotion of her bodily heart.

Secondly, Mary kept all these things in her spiritual heart, that is, in the noblest part of her soul, in the inmost recesses of her mind. All the faculties of her soul were constantly applied to contemplating and adoring everything that took place in the life of her Beloved Son, down to the very smallest details.

Thirdly, Our Lady kept all these things in her divine Heart, that is, in her son, Jesus, who was the mind of her mind and the heart of her heart. He in turn kept them for her and recalled them to her mind when necessary, that she might feed herself in contemplation upon the mysteries of his life, rendering them due honor and adoration, and repeating them to the holy apostles and disciples, who were to preach them to the faithful.

Prayer

St. Louis de Montfort

A Treatise on the True Devotion to the Blessed Virgin

Latin

Tuus totus ego sum, et omnia mea tua sunt; O virgo gloriosa, super omnia benedicta, ponam te ut signaculum super cor meum, quia fortis est ut mors dilectio tua.

English

I am altogether yours, and all that I have belongs to you; O glorious Virgin, blessed above all created things! I will put you as a seal upon my heart, because your love is as strong as death.

Implore that good Mother to lend you her heart, that you may receive her son there with the same dispositions as her own.

—ST. LOUIS DE MONTFORT

✴

A Sword Will Pierce Your Soul

Poem

G.K. Chesterton

From "The Queen of Seven Swords"

I had dreamed of a desolate land, deformed to its crooked
skyline
As if the round earth itself could be bent out of shape in its
shame,
Its plants stamped flat like a pattern, by marching of more
than mammoths,
Huge things, more naked and nameless; too old or new for a
name.

And I knew what Spirit had passed, who is vast beyond
meaning or measure,
The blank in the brain of the whirlwind, the hollow, the
hungry thing,
The Nothing that swells and desire, the void that devours and
dismembers,
In the heart of barbarian armies or the idle hours of a king.

Low light on the flat-topped hills, like headless creatures of
chaos,

Long shadows striping the slime, like ghosts laid flat in the grave,
Low clouds lying flattened and spread, as if heaven itself lay prostrate;
And I looked on the world-wide waste; and I said, "There is none to save."

I knew not if time out of mind, last night or now or to-morrow,
Had broken that obscene dawn; on the strange, scarred hills I trod,
I saw on their breaking terraces, cracking and sinking for ever,
One shrine rise blackened and broken; like a last cry to God.

One gold on the roof hung ragged as scales of a dragon dropping,
The gross green weeds of the desert had spawned on the painted wood:
But erect in the earth's despair and arisen against heaven interceding,
Whose name is Cause of Our Joy, in the doorway of death, she stood.

The Seven Swords of her Sorrow held out their hilts like a challenge,
The blast of that stunning silence as a sevenfold trumpet blew

Majestic in more than gold, girt round with a glory of iron,
The hub of her wheel of weapons; with a truth beyond torture,
  true.

Scripture

Luke 2:22–35

When the time came for their purification according to the law of Moses, they brought him up to Jerusalem to present him to the Lord (as it is written in the law of the Lord, "Every firstborn male shall be designated as holy to the Lord"), and they offered a sacrifice according to what is stated in the law of the Lord, "a pair of turtledoves or two young pigeons."

Now there was a man in Jerusalem whose name was Simeon; this man was righteous and devout, looking forward to the consolation of Israel, and the Holy Spirit rested on him. It had been revealed to him by the Holy Spirit that he would not see death before he had seen the Lord's Messiah. Guided by the Spirit, Simeon came into the temple; and when the parents brought in the child Jesus, to do for him what was customary under the law, Simeon took him in his arms and praised God, saying,

"Master, now you are dismissing your servant in peace,
  according to your word;
for my eyes have seen your salvation,
  which you have prepared in the presence of all peoples,

a light for revelation to the Gentiles
and for glory to your people Israel."

And the child's father and mother were amazed at what was being said about him. Then Simeon blessed them and said to his mother Mary, "This child is destined for the falling and the rising of many in Israel, and to be a sign that will be opposed so that the inner thoughts of many will be revealed—and a sword will pierce your own soul too."

Reflection

Bishop Barron
The Pivotal Players

Simeon's prophecy to Mary that a sword would pierce her own soul comes to pass in the excruciating (*ex cruce*, "from the cross") sufferings of her son during his Passion and Crucifixion. Indeed, in the Gospel of John, we hear that Jesus' mother was beside him to the very end (John 19:25–26).

Michelangelo's iconic *Pietà* depicts Mary cradling her son in her arms after his death on the cross. And one of the most extraordinary features of the *Pietà*, from a purely structural or compositional standpoint, is how Michelangelo managed to make the figures of Jesus and Mary look so natural and elegant together, despite the fact that what is being presented is a woman supporting the body of an adult man on her lap. In fact, Mary's body is significantly larger than that of Jesus. She contains him. In the wonderful words of Sr. Wendy Beckett, she is like a great mountain, and his body is like a river flowing down.

According to the Gospel accounts, Mary, having given birth to Jesus, placed him in a manger, the place where the animals eat. At the climax of his life, Jesus would become food for the life of the world. Therefore, Michelangelo depicts Mary's left hand in a gesture of offering, as though she is presenting him as a gift; her right hand supports him but touches him only indirectly, through her garment. Both are Eucharistic references. The Church continually offers the Body of Jesus under the forms of bread and wine, and when the priest shows the Blessed Sacrament, he touches the monstrance only through a veil. Keep in mind that this sculpture was intended to be an altarpiece—that is to say, something closely associated with the celebration of the Mass. What we see in the *Pietà* is what we see at the Mass—namely, the offering of the body of the crucified Jesus for the life of the world.

Catechism

529

The *presentation of Jesus in the temple* shows him to be the firstborn Son who belongs to the Lord (see Luke 2:22–39; Exod. 13:2, 12–13). With Simeon and Anna, all Israel awaits its *encounter* with the Savior—the name given to this event in the

Byzantine tradition. Jesus is recognized as the long-expected Messiah, the "light to the nations" and the "glory of Israel," but also "a sign that is spoken against." The sword of sorrow predicted for Mary announces Christ's perfect and unique oblation on the cross that will impart the salvation God had "prepared in the presence of all peoples."

Reflection

St. John Henry Newman
Meditations and Devotions

Mary is the "Regina Martyrum," the Queen of Martyrs. Why is she so called? She who never had any blow, or wound, or other injury to her consecrated person. How can she be exalted over those whose bodies suffered the most ruthless violences and the keenest torments or our Lord's sake? She is, indeed, Queen of All Saints, of those who walk with Christ "in white, for they are worthy" (Rev. 3:4); but how of those "who had been slaughtered for the word of God and for the testimony they had given" (Rev. 6:9)?

To answer this question, it must be recollected that the pains of the soul may be as fierce as those of the body. Bad men who are now in hell, and the elect of God who are in purgatory, are suffering only in their souls, for their bodies are still in the dust; yet how severe is that suffering! And perhaps most people who have lived long can bear witness in their own persons to a sharpness of distress which was like a sword cutting them, to a weight and force of sorrow which seemed to throw them down, though bodily pain there was none.

What an overwhelming horror it must have been for the Blessed Mary to witness the Passion and Crucifixion of her son! Her anguish was, as holy Simeon had announced to her, at the time of that Son's presentation in the temple, a sword piercing her soul. If our Lord himself could not bear the prospect of what was before him, and was covered in the thought of it with a bloody sweat, his soul thus acting upon His body, does not this show how great mental pain can be? And would it have been wonderful though Mary's head and heart had given way as she stood under his cross?

Thus she is most truly the Queen of *Martyrs*.

Prayer

St. John Henry Newman
Meditations and Devotions

O Lord Jesus Christ, God and man, grant, we beseech Thee, that Thy dear Mother Mary, whose soul the sword pierced in the hour of Thy passion, may intercede for us, now, and in the hour of our death, through Thine own merits, O Savior of the world, who with the Father and the Holy Spirit livest and reignest, God, world without end. Amen.

Stabat Mater dolorosa,
Iuxta Crucem lacrimosa,
Dum pendebat Filius.

At the cross her station keeping,
Stood the mournful Mother weeping,
Close to Jesus to the last.

—"STABAT MATER"

The Role of a Mother

Poem

Pope St. John Paul II
"Her Amazement at Her Only Child"

Light piercing, gradually, everyday events;
a woman's eyes, hands
used to them since childhood.
Then brightness flared, too huge for simple days,
and hands clasped when the words lost their space.

In that little town, my son, where they knew us together,
you called me mother; but no one had eyes to see
the astounding events as they took place day by day.
Your life became the life of the poor
in your wish to be with them through the work of your hands.

I knew: the light that lingered in ordinary things,
like a spark sheltered under the skin of our days—
the light was you;
it did not come from me.

And I had more of you in that luminous silence
than I had of you as the fruit of my body, my blood.

Scripture

Luke 2:41–51

Now every year his parents went to Jerusalem for the festival of the Passover. And when he was twelve years old, they went up as usual for the festival. When the festival was ended and they started to return, the boy Jesus stayed behind in Jerusalem, but his parents did not know it. Assuming that he was in the group of travelers, they went a day's journey. Then they started to look for him among their relatives and friends. When they did not find him, they returned to Jerusalem to search for him. After three days they found him in the temple, sitting among the teachers, listening to them and asking them questions. And all who heard him were amazed at his understanding and his answers. When his parents saw him they were astonished; and his mother said to him, "Child, why have you treated us like this? Look, your father and I have been searching for you in great anxiety." He said to them, "Why were you searching for me? Did you not know that I must be in my Father's house?" But they did not understand what he said to them. Then he went down with them and came to Nazareth, and was obedient to them. His mother treasured all these things in her heart.

Reflection

Bishop Barron

Proclaiming the Power of Christ

In Luke's Gospel, we hear the instructive story of Mary and Joseph finding the child Jesus in the temple. Looking desperately for their lost son over the course of three days, enduring sleepless nights, envisioning over and again the worst possible scenarios, Mary and Joseph must have experienced the darkest of emotions. Thus, when they finally track him down in the temple precincts, debating with the elders, they are understandably exasperated. Mary chastises him: "Child, why have you treated us like this? Look, your father and I have been searching for you in great anxiety." But Jesus appears oblivious to their frantic emotions and replies with devastating brevity: "Why were you searching for me? Did you not know that I must be in my Father's house?" (Luke 2:48–49).

Despite the intense feelings of his mother, a child finds his place in the temple. What is being dramatically called into question is the primacy of emotion and personal feeling in determining a child's life. What matters above all, the Bible teaches over and again, is to find one's mission—and nothing, not even the strongest familial bonds, ought to obstruct that task. Sentiment, however legitimate and understandable, devolves into self-regarding sentimentality when it takes primacy over the purposes of God.

With this counterintuitive story of Mary in mind, let us consider a few of Jesus' own choice comments about families. When a prospective disciple asks for leave to bury his father—an act of piety as highly prized in first-century Jewish culture as it is in ours—Jesus replies with a bluntness that we could only characterize as deeply insensitive: "Follow me, and let the dead bury their own dead" (Matt. 8:22). When a woman cries out enthusiastically, "Blessed is the womb that bore you and the breasts that nursed you," Jesus fires back, "Blessed rather are those who hear the word of God and obey it" (Luke 11:27–28). On still another occasion, when his disciples say, "Your mother and your brothers and sisters are outside, asking for you," Jesus replies, "Who are my mother and my brothers? . . . Whoever does the will of God is my brother and sister and mother" (Mark 3:32–33, 35). And most devastatingly: "Do not think that I have come to bring peace to the earth; I have not come to bring peace, but a sword. For I have come to set a man against his father, and a daughter against her mother" (Matt. 10:34–35).

What could these blistering and provocative comments possibly mean? Jesus insists upon the proper prioritization of spiritual values. To listen to the Word of God, to follow after the Messiah, to do the will of the Lord are the supreme goods, and they must not be compromised by, or rendered secondary to, any other good. In order to test his disciples, therefore, Jesus purposely contrasts the Gospel call to those most emotionally precious and ethically compelling values that obtain within families. Even these—especially these—must give way before the demands of God. Nowhere is this principle more succinctly summarized than in this saying of the Lord: "Whoever loves father or mother more than me is not worthy of me; and whoever loves son or daughter more than me is not worthy of me" (Matt. 10:37).

John Paul II said often that the family is meant to be an *ecclesiola*—a little church. This means that the family is the forum in which the worship of God is the supreme value and the discernment of mission is the supreme task. Parents should realize that their first responsibility is to shape their children not so much for worldly accomplishment but for God's work. And they should, therefore, cultivate the emotional detachment necessary to these ends—and demonstrate the quality so clearly on display in Mary: the willingness to let their children remain in the temple.

Catechism

534

The *finding of Jesus in the temple* is the only event that breaks the silence of the Gospels about the hidden years of Jesus (see Luke 2:41–52). Here Jesus lets us catch a glimpse of the mystery of his total consecration to a mission that flows from his divine sonship: "Did you not know that I must be about my Father's work?" (Luke 2:49). Mary and Joseph did not understand these words, but they accepted them in faith. Mary "kept all these things in her heart" during the years Jesus remained hidden in the silence of an ordinary life.

Reflection

St. Augustine
Letter

Did your Commander not have an earthly Mother? When in the midst of his heavenly tasks it was announced to him that she was there, he answered: "'Who is my mother, and who are my brothers?' And pointing to his disciples," he said that no one belonged to his kindred except the one who would do the will of His Father (Matt. 12:47–50; see Mark 3:32–35; Luke 8:20–21). To be sure, he graciously included Mary herself in this number, for she was doing the will of his Father. Thus, the name of mother that they had announced to him as his private and personal possession he rejected, because it was an earthly name when compared to heavenly kinship, and, referring that same heavenly kinship to his Apostles, he showed again the bond of relationship by which that Virgin was bound to him, together with all the saints. And lest error should find some support from that salutary authority with which he taught us to despise earthly affection for our parents by saying, as some did, that he had no mother, he charged his disciples on another occasion not to say that they had a father on earth (Matt. 23:9), but just as it is certain that they had fathers, so he showed that he had a mother, while at the same time he gave his disciples an example of contemning such relationship by his rejection of earthly kindred.

Prayer

Pope St. John Paul II

Pastores Dabo Vobis

O Mary,
Mother of Jesus Christ and Mother of priests,
accept this title which we bestow on you
to celebrate your motherhood
and to contemplate with you the priesthood
of your Son and of your sons,
O holy Mother of God.

O Mother of Christ,
to the Messiah-priest you gave a body of flesh
through the anointing of the Holy Spirit
for the salvation of the poor and the contrite of heart;
guard priests in your heart and in the Church,
O Mother of the Savior.

O Mother of Faith,
you accompanied to the temple the Son of Man,
the fulfillment of the promises given to the fathers;

give to the Father for his glory
the priests of your Son,
O Ark of the Covenant.

O Mother of the Church,
in the midst of the disciples in the upper room
you prayed to the Spirit
for the new people and their shepherds;
obtain for the Order of Presbyters
a full measure of gifts,
O Queen of the Apostles.

O Mother of Jesus Christ,
you were with him at the beginning
of his life and mission,
you sought the Master among the crowd,
you stood beside him when he was lifted
up from the earth
consumed as the one eternal sacrifice,
and you had John, your son, near at hand;
accept from the beginning those
who have been called,
protect their growth,
in their life and ministry accompany
your sons,
O Mother of Priests.
Amen.

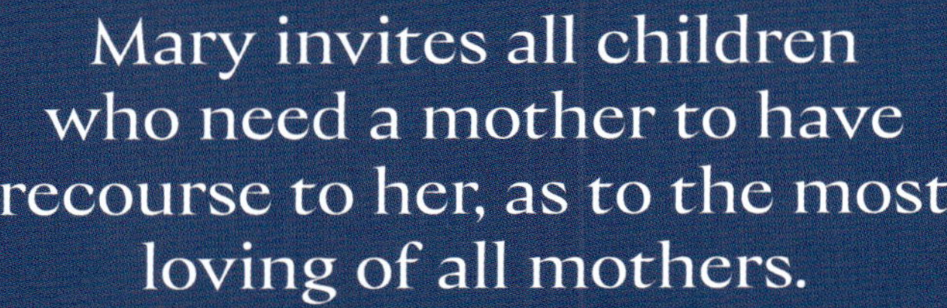

Mary invites all children who need a mother to have recourse to her, as to the most loving of all mothers.

—ST. ALPHONSUS LIGUORI

Hymn

Alma Redemptoris Mater

(Sung from the First Sunday of Advent to the Feast of the Presentation)

Latin

Alma Redemptoris Mater, quae pervia caeli
porta manes, et stella maris, succurre cadenti,
surgere qui curat, populo: tu quae genuisti,
natura mirante, tuum sanctum Genitorem,
Virgo prius ac posterius, Gabrielis ab ore
sumens illud Ave, peccatorum miserere.

English

Loving mother of the Redeemer,
gate of heaven, star of the sea,
assist your people who have fallen yet strive to rise again.
To the wonderment of nature you bore your Creator,
yet remained a virgin after as before.
You who received Gabriel's joyful greeting,
have pity on us poor sinners.

III.
Mother *of the* Church

✶ The Mother

Sally Read

A man once hypothesized that Mary ran from the Cross
to save her own skin. Surely he was blind to these things:
Christ as a blasted tree, fused black against the sky—
scourged, slashed, stabbed—and his mother as the deep roots
beneath him. How could she go? She was the earthed
wire of his agony, routing his pain to the earth's marrow:
the ground will never stop singing, nor our bones,
if they'll listen. Our children hurt and they cry;
we carry their grief in our frames like a new
kind of gravity. Understand, you who doubt this love,
or the grit to bear it: the long fields are ready for running,
and many do run. But like those fields seeded thoroughly
with yellow everlastings, she is the ground of his life,
the shell of his sounding. There is nowhere else she could be.

Do Whatever He Tells You

Poem

Justin Mulcahy, CP

"Mary the Dawn"

Mary the Dawn, Christ the Perfect Day;
Mary the Gate, Christ the Heavenly Way!
Mary the Root, Christ the Mystic Vine;
Mary the Grape, Christ the Sacred Wine!
Mary the Wheat, Christ the Living-Bread;
Mary the Stem, Christ the Rose blood-red!
Mary the Font, Christ the Cleansing Flood;
Mary the Cup, Christ the Saving Blood!
Mary the Temple, Christ the Temple's Lord;
Mary the Shrine, Christ the God adored!
Mary the Beacon, Christ the Haven's Rest;
Mary the Mirror, Christ the Vision Blest!
Mary the Mother, Christ the Mother's Son;
By all things blest while endless ages run.

Scripture

John 2:1–12

On the third day there was a wedding in Cana of Galilee, and the mother of Jesus was there. Jesus and his disciples had also been invited to the wedding. When the wine gave out, the mother of Jesus said to him, "They have no wine." And Jesus said to her, "Woman, what concern is that to you and to me? My hour has not yet come." His mother said to the servants, "Do whatever he tells you." Now standing there were six stone water jars for the Jewish rites of purification, each holding twenty or thirty gallons. Jesus said to them, "Fill the jars with water." And they filled them up to the brim. He said to them, "Now draw some out, and take it to the chief steward." So they took it. When the steward tasted the water that had become wine, and did not know where it came from (though the servants who had drawn the water knew), the steward called the bridegroom and said to him, "Everyone serves the good wine first, and then the inferior wine after the guests have become drunk. But you have kept the good wine until now." Jesus did this, the first of his signs, in Cana of Galilee, and revealed his glory; and his disciples believed in him.

After this he went down to Capernaum with his mother, his brothers, and his disciples; and they remained there a few days.

Reflection

Bishop Barron

The Priority of Christ

Throughout the Old Testament, the motif of the wedding is used to symbolize the marriage of God and his people as well as the good cheer that obtains when human beings come together in love. It is accordingly a particularly apt expression of the overcoming of the sundering of sin. Thus, it is no accident that in the context of John's Gospel, Jesus' first public "sign" takes place at a wedding feast, for he himself is the marriage of divinity and humanity.

We hear that the disciples of Jesus—presumably at this point Andrew, Simon Peter, Philip, Nathanael, and the disciple whom Jesus loved—were invited to the wedding along with the Lord himself and his mother. The presence of both the disciples and the mother are key. In calling disciples to himself, Jesus had already inaugurated the gathering of his people (eventually the Twelve will be seen as evocative of the twelve tribes of Israel), and so their presence signals the novelty and future purpose of Jesus' ministry. Mary is a rich and multivalent symbolic figure in all of the Gospels. In Luke's infancy narrative, she emerges as the spokesperson for ancient Israel, speaking, in her Magnificat, in the words and cadences of Hannah; and as the recipient of an angelic announcement of a miraculous birth, she calls to mind not only Hannah but also Sarah and the mother of Samson as well. In Matthew's Christmas account, she is compelled to go into exile in Egypt and is then called back to her home, recapitulating thereby the journey of Israel from slavery to freedom. She is thus the symbolic embodiment of faithful and patient Israel, longing for deliverance.

In John's Gospel, she is, above all, mother—the physical mother of Jesus and, through him, the mother of all who would come to new life in him. As mother of the Lord, she is, once again, Israel, that entire series of events and system of ideas from which Jesus emerged and in terms of which he alone becomes intelligible. Hans Urs von Balthasar comments in the same vein that Mary effectively awakened the messianic consciousness of Jesus through her recounting of the story of Israel to her son. So in the Cana narrative, Mary will speak the pain and the hope of the chosen people, scattered and longing for union.

We hear that in the course of the wedding celebration "the wine gave out" (John 2:3). In an era when such parties lasted upward of several days, this was not a minor difficulty. With the wine depleted, the spirit of conviviality would dissipate, the celebration would wind down quickly, and the hosts, as well as the bride and groom, would be profoundly embarrassed. Noticing the difficulty, the mother of Jesus said to him, "They have no wine" (John 2:3).

Let us press ahead with a symbolic reading of this iconic episode. Wine—that which changes, uplifts, and enlivens the consciousness, that which produces good feeling and good fellowship—evokes the Spirit of God, the divine life. When we are linked to that infinite source, when we partake freely of it, we are brought to personal joy and a deep sense of community connection. It is the elixir that makes of human life a communal celebration; it is the condition for the possibility of the gathering. To be in sin is nothing other than to be sundered from that source and hence to fall into a depression of the spirit, a listlessness and loneliness. When Mary quietly suggests to Jesus that the wedding party has run out of wine, she is ancient Israel speaking to its God, reminding him that the people have run out of joy, purpose, and connection to one another, that they have become dry bones with no life. She is taking up the lament of so many of the Hebrew prophets and sages: "How long, O Lord?"

What follows is the most puzzling part of the story: Jesus' seemingly cold distancing of himself from this reasonable request of his mother. "Woman, what concern is that to you and to me? My hour has not yet come" (John 2:4). First, his addressing her as "woman" should not be construed as a mark of disrespect; rather, it should be interpreted as a densely textured symbolic act. Eve, in the Old Testament context, is the woman par excellence; Mary is presented here as the New Eve, the new representative of the human race, with whom God is seeking union. As is fitting in this Cana setting, the theme of human bride and divine bridegroom is being hinted at. But if she is the

Woman with whom God seeks union, why the aloof and off-putting words? The best explanation, in my judgment, is that this is a narrative device that serves to highlight the importance of Jesus' "hour" and shows the relation between what he does at Cana and what will transpire in that hour. Like "the third day," "hour" is code for the Paschal Mystery, Jesus' passage through death to life. In that event, God will effect the perfect marriage between himself and the human race, for he will enter into the most intimate union with us, embracing even death itself and leading us into the bridal chamber of the divine life. Thus, the exchange with Mary brings to our attention the ultimate purpose and correct symbolic setting for the action that Jesus will perform for the humble bride and groom of Cana.

Unfazed by her son's response, Mary says to the *diakonoi* (the table servers), "Do whatever he tells you" (John 2:5). Once again, this is Israel who is speaking. The rupture between God and humanity is irreparable from the human side and through human effort. The dysfunction into which men and women have fallen is like an addiction or an obsession: any attempt on their part to overcome the difficulty will only sink them deeper into it. Therefore, the proper attitude in the presence of the saving God is obedience and acquiescence, imitating his moves, responding to his commands, doing whatever he tells us.

Catechism

721–725

Mary, the all-holy ever-virgin Mother of God, is the masterwork of the mission of the Son and the Spirit in the fullness of time. For the first time in the plan of salvation and because his Spirit had prepared her, the Father found the *dwelling place* where his Son and his Spirit could dwell among men. In this sense the Church's Tradition has often read the most beautiful texts on wisdom in relation to Mary (see Prov. 8:1–9:6; Sir. 24). Mary is acclaimed and represented in the liturgy as the "Seat of Wisdom."

In her, the "wonders of God" that the Spirit was to fulfill in Christ and the Church began to be manifested:

The Holy Spirit *prepared* Mary by his grace. It was fitting that the mother of him in whom "the whole fullness of deity dwells bodily" (Col. 2:9) should herself be "full of grace." She was, by sheer grace, conceived without sin as the most humble of creatures, the most capable of welcoming the inexpressible gift of the Almighty. It was quite correct for the angel Gabriel to greet her as the "Daughter of Zion": "Rejoice" (see Zeph. 3:14; Zech. 2:10). It is the thanksgiving of the whole People of God, and thus of the Church, which Mary in her canticle (see Luke 1:46–55) lifts up to the Father in the Holy Spirit while carrying within her the eternal Son.

In Mary, the Holy Spirit *fulfills* the plan of the Father's loving goodness. Through the Holy Spirit, the Virgin conceives and gives birth to the Son of God. By the Holy Spirit's power and her faith, her virginity became uniquely fruitful (see Luke 1:26–38; Rom. 4:18–21; Gal. 4:26–28).

In Mary, the Holy Spirit *manifests* the Son of the Father, now become the Son of the Virgin. She is the burning bush of the definitive theophany. Filled with the Holy Spirit she makes the Word visible in the humility of his flesh. It is to the poor and the first representatives of the gentiles that she makes him known (see Luke 1:15–19; Matt. 2:11).

Finally, through Mary, the Holy Spirit begins to bring men, the objects of God's merciful love (see Luke 2:14), *into communion* with Christ. And the humble are always the first to accept him: shepherds, magi, Simeon and Anna, the bride and groom at Cana, and the first disciples.

Reflection

Second Vatican Council

Lumen Gentium

There is but one Mediator as we know from the words of the apostle, "for there is one God and one mediator of God and men, the man Christ Jesus, who gave himself a redemption for all" (1 Tim. 2:5–6). The maternal duty of Mary toward men in no wise obscures or diminishes this unique mediation of Christ, but rather shows His power. For all the salvific influence of the Blessed Virgin on men originates, not from some inner necessity, but from the divine pleasure. It flows forth from the superabundance of the merits of Christ, rests on His mediation, depends entirely on it and draws all its power from it. In no way does it impede, but rather does it foster the immediate union of the faithful with Christ.

Predestined from eternity by that decree of divine providence which determined the incarnation of the Word to be the Mother of God, the Blessed Virgin was on this earth the virgin Mother of the Redeemer, and above all others and in a singular way the generous associate and humble handmaid of the Lord. She conceived, brought forth, and nourished Christ. She presented Him to the Father in the temple, and was united with Him by compassion as He died on the Cross. In this singular way she cooperated by her obedience, faith, hope, and burning charity in the work of the Savior in giving back supernatural life to souls. Wherefore she is our mother in the order of grace.

This maternity of Mary in the order of grace began with the consent which she gave in faith at the Annunciation and which she sustained without wavering beneath the cross, and lasts until the eternal fulfillment of all the elect. Taken up to heaven she did not lay aside this salvific duty, but by her constant intercession continued to bring us the gifts of eternal salvation.[1] By her maternal charity, she cares for the brethren of her Son, who still journey on earth surrounded by dangers and cultics, until they are led into the happiness of their true home. Therefore the Blessed Virgin is invoked by the Church under the titles of Advocate, Auxiliatrix, Adjutrix, and Mediatrix.[2] This, however, is to be so understood that it neither takes away from nor adds anything to the dignity and efficaciousness of Christ the one Mediator.[3]

For no creature could ever be counted as equal with the Incarnate Word and Redeemer. Just as the priesthood of Christ is shared in various ways both by the ministers and by the faithful, and as the one goodness of God is really communicated in different ways to His creatures, so also the unique mediation of the Redeemer does not exclude but rather gives rise to a manifold cooperation which is but a sharing in this one source.

The Church does not hesitate to profess this subordinate role of Mary. It knows it through unfailing experience of it and commends it to the hearts of the faithful, so that encouraged by this maternal help they may the more intimately adhere to the Mediator and Redeemer.

1. See Kleutgen, textus reformatus De mysterio Verbi incarnati, cap. IV: Mansi 53, 290. See S. Andreas Cret., In nat. Mariac, sermo 4: Patrologia Graeca 97, 865 A. S. Germanus Constantinop., In annunt. Deiparae: PG 98, 321 BC. In dorm. Deiparae, III: col. 361 D. S. Io. Damascenus, In dorm. B. V. Mariae, Hom. 1, 8: PG 96, 712 BC–713 A.

2. See Leo XIII, Litt. Encycl. Adiutricem populi, 5 sept. 1895: ASS 15 (1895-96), p. 303. S. Pius X, Litt. Encycl. Ad diem illum, 2 febr. 1904: Acta, I, p. 154 Denz. 1978 a (3370). Pius XI, Litt. Encycl. Miserentissimus, 8 maii 1928: AAS 20 (1928) p. 178. Pius XII, Nuntius Radioph., 13 maii 1946: AAS 38 (1946) p. 266.

3. S. Ambrosius, Epist. 63: Patrologia Latina 16, 1218.

Prayer

St. Louis de Montfort

The Secret of Mary

Hail Mary, beloved daughter of the Eternal Father! Hail Mary, admirable mother of the Son! Hail Mary, most faithful Spouse of the Holy Spirit! . . .

May the light of your faith dispel the darkness of my mind; may your deep humility take the place of my pride; may your sublime contemplation arrest the distraction of my wandering imagination; may your continual sight of God fill my memory with his Presence; may the fire of the charity of your heart inflame the lukewarmness and coldness of my own; may your virtues take the place of my sins; may your merits be my ornament, and make up for all that is wanting in me before God. Lastly, most dear and well-beloved mother, grant, if it may be, that I may have no other spirit but your spirit, to know Jesus Christ, and his divine and blessed will; that I may have no other soul but your soul, to praise and glorify the Lord; that I may have no other heart but your heart, to love God with a pure and burning love like yours.

Only a few words from the Virgin Mary have come down to us in the Gospels. But these few words are like heavy grains of pure gold. When they melt in the ardor of loving meditation, they more than suffice to bathe our entire lives in a luminous golden glow.

—ST. TERESA BENEDICTA OF THE CROSS (EDITH STEIN)

Perpetual Virgin

Poem

Jessica Powers
"Total Virgin"

"She was virgin even of herself"—Père Francois, OCD

In a house of mirrors that coveted her image
she never walked
with her own beauty
nor made a feast of her goodness,
inviting friends from the far and wide.
She never sat down with her own innocence
to dialogue together,
nor called a stranger in
to sit at her hearth and be glorified.

She was a maiden promised to one lover
whom she was always seeking.
Though he hid in her heartbeat and settled himself
behind her breath,
he was distance, too. Journeys dwindled to places
beside her own, and miles melted beneath

her steps of wanting. She could by-pass all
meadows that trap us with their poisonous flowers
and their soliciting pools
and winding lanes that skirt the only death.

She was out on a road alone, hastening onward,
gathering all as a gift, the small and great
fragments of mystery and reality.
Everything was for Him, even her own being.
Since love marks neither measurement or weight
she carried all, without touching or tasting.

Life which comes as a virgin to us all,
most safely came to her.
Time, when she passed, remained inviolate.

Scripture

Matthew 13:54–57

He came to his hometown and began to teach the people in their synagogue, so that they were astounded and said, "Where did this man get this wisdom and these deeds of power? Is not this the carpenter's son? Is not his mother called Mary? And are not his brothers James and Joseph and Simon and Judas? And are not all his sisters with us? Where then did this man get all this?" And they took offense at him.

Reflection

Bishop Barron
Light from Light

The virginity of Mary seems fitting for a number of reasons. First, it indicates, as clearly as possible, that God is involved in the coming to be of Jesus. Though human cooperation, at both the physical and moral level, is required, the Incarnation would not have happened without a gracious divine initiative. Further, it signals that the Incarnation involves not simply a revolution in the moral and spiritual order but an entirely new creation. Just as Adam, on the biblical telling, is made through the direct causality of God, so the New Adam is made *de novo*, and not in the ordinary course.

Finally, the virginity of Mary is a sign of the purity and completeness of her devotion to God, making her a fit vessel for the divine Messiah. She becomes mother in the physical order, though she is given utterly over to God; she is, as classical Christian piety would have it, spouse of the Holy Spirit. All of this, one might argue, is summed up in the greeting that the angel gives Mary at the Annunciation, the most sublime offered to any human being in the biblical tradition: *Kecharitomene*, "full of grace."

Catechism

499–501

The deepening of faith in the virginal motherhood led the Church to confess Mary's real and perpetual virginity even in the act of giving birth to the Son of God made man.[1] In fact, Christ's birth "did not diminish his mother's virginal integrity but sanctified it."[2] And so the liturgy of the Church celebrates Mary as *Aeiparthenos*, the "Ever-virgin."[3]

Against this doctrine the objection is sometimes raised that the Bible mentions brothers and sisters of Jesus (see Mark 3:31–35, 6:3; 1 Cor. 9:5; Gal. 1:19). The Church has always understood these passages as not referring to other children of the Virgin Mary. In fact James and Joseph, "brothers of Jesus," are the sons of another Mary, a disciple of Christ, whom St. Matthew significantly calls "the other Mary" (Matt. 13:55, 28:1; see Matt. 27:56). They are close relations of Jesus, according to an Old Testament expression (see Gen. 13:8, 14:16, 29:15).

Jesus is Mary's only son, but her spiritual motherhood extends to all men whom indeed he came to save: "The Son whom she brought forth is he whom God placed as the first-born among many brethren, that is, the faithful in whose generation and formulation she cooperates with a mother's love."[4]

---

1. See Denzinger-Schönmetzer 291, 294, 427, 442, 503, 571, 1880.
2. *Lumen Gentium* 57.
3. See *LG* 52.
4. *LG* 63; see John 19:26–27; Rom. 8:29; Rev. 12:17.

Reflection

St. Jerome

The Perpetual Virginity of Blessed Mary

As we do not deny what is written, so we do reject what is not written. We believe that God was born of the Virgin, because we read it. That Mary was married after she brought forth, we do not believe, because we do not read it. Nor do we say this to condemn marriage, for virginity itself is the fruit of marriage; but because when we are dealing with saints we must not judge rashly. If we adopt possibility as the standard of judgment, we might maintain that Joseph had several wives because Abraham had, and so had Jacob, and that the Lord's brethren were the issue of those wives, an invention which some hold with a rashness which springs from audacity not from piety. You say that Mary did not continue a virgin: I claim still more, that Joseph himself on account of Mary was a virgin, so that from a virgin wedlock a virgin son was born. For if as a holy man he does not come under the imputation of fornication, and it is nowhere written that he had another wife, but was the guardian of Mary whom he was supposed to have to wife rather than her husband, the conclusion is that he who was thought worthy to be called father of the Lord, remained a virgin.

Prayer

The Liturgy of St. John Chrysostom

Commemorating our most holy, most pure, most blessed and glorious Lady, Mary ever Virgin and Mother of God, with all the saints, let us commend ourselves and one another and our whole life to Christ our God; for to you, O Lord, belongs all glory, all honor, and all worship, now and forever. Amen.

A Virgin conceiving, a Virgin bearing, a Virgin pregnant, a Virgin bringing forth, a Virgin perpetual. Why do you wonder at this, O man? It was fitting for God to be born thus, when he deigned to become man.

—ST. AUGUSTINE

Here Is Your Mother

Poem

St. Teresa Benedicta of the Cross (Edith Stein)
"Juxta Crucem tecum stare!" (Beneath the Cross I Stood with You)

Today I stood with you beneath the Cross,
And felt more clearly than I ever did
That you became our Mother only there.
Even an earthly mother faithfully
Seeks to fulfill the last will of her son.
But you became the handmaid of the Lord;
The life and being of the God made Man
Was perfectly inscribed in your own life.
So you could take your own into your heart,
And with the lifeblood of your bitter pains
You purchased life anew for every soul.
You know us all, our wounds, our imperfections;
But you know also the celestial radiance
Which your Son's love would shed on us in Heaven.
Thus carefully you guide our faltering footsteps,
No price too high for you to lead us to our goal.
But those whom you have chosen for companions

To stand with you round the eternal throne,
They here must stand with you beneath the Cross,
And with the lifeblood of their bitter pains
Must purchase heavenly glory for those souls
Whom God's own Son entrusted to their care.

Scripture

John 19:25–27

Standing near the cross of Jesus were his mother, and his mother's sister, Mary the wife of Clopas, and Mary Magdalene. When Jesus saw his mother and the disciple whom he loved standing beside her, he said to his mother, "Woman, here is your son." Then he said to the disciple, "Here is your mother." And from that hour the disciple took her into his own home.

Reflection

Bishop Barron

Catholicism

In so many depictions of the Crucifixion, two figures, Mary and John—his mother and the disciple whom he loved—stand by the cross. When everyone else had fled, they remained. Henri de Lubac said that the Church was already there in its fullness when those two people stood with the dying Jesus. The essence of the Church is not a matter of numbers or global influence;

it is a participation in those two archetypal figures, the mother and the son.

As he was dying on the cross, Jesus looked to them, and he said to Mary, "Woman, here is your son," and then to John, "Here is your mother" (John 19:26–27). We are told that "from that hour the disciple took her into his own home" (John 19:27). This text supports an ancient tradition that the Apostle John took Mary with him when he traveled to Ephesus in Asia Minor and that both ended their days in that city. Indeed, on the top of a high hill overlooking the Aegean Sea, just outside Ephesus, there is a modest dwelling that tradition holds to be the house of Mary.

What we see on display here at the cross is Mary's role as Mother of the Church—a further implication of her status as Mother of God. If she is the one through whom Christ was born, and if the Church is Christ's Mystical Body, then she must be, in a very real sense, the Mother of the Church. She is the one through whom Jesus continues to be born in the hearts of those who believe. This is not to confuse her with the Savior, but it is to insist on her mission as intercessor. At the close of the great prayer the Hail Mary, we Catholics ask Mary to pray for us "now and at the hour of our death," signaling that throughout one's life Mary is the privileged channel through which the grace of Christ flows into the Mystical Body. Here, the principle of God's noncompetitive transcendence is apposite. God is not threatened by his creation. On the contrary, he delights in drawing secondary causes into the dense complexity of his providential plan, granting to them the honor of cooperating with him and his designs. The handmaid of the Lord, who is the Mother of the Church, is the humblest of these humble instruments—and therefore the most effective.

Hans Urs von Balthasar has argued that the Marian form is the matrix of all Church life and ministry. He means that her *fiat* ("let it be with me according to your word") opens up the creaturely space within which God can work. Mary's freedom, surrendered utterly to God, becomes the condition for the possibility of all forms of mission and outreach in the life of the Church. The Petrine ministry of office, the Johannine ministry of prayer and contemplation, and the Pauline ministry of theologizing and evangelization—the kingly, priestly, and prophetic offices, if you will—are all finally reducible to the Marian form. This is why in much medieval and early modern Christian art, Mary is often depicted gathering all manner of life under her protective mantle. This is not sentimental piety, but a robust presentation of Mary, the Mother of the Church.

Catechism

2673–2677

In prayer the Holy Spirit unites us to the person of the only Son, in his glorified humanity, through which and in which our filial prayer unites us in the Church with the Mother of Jesus (see Acts 1:14).

Mary gave her consent in faith at the Annunciation and maintained it without hesitation at the foot of the Cross. Ever since, her motherhood has extended to the brothers and sisters of her Son "who still journey on earth surrounded by dangers and difficulties."[1] Jesus, the only mediator, is the way of our prayer; Mary, his mother and ours, is wholly transparent to him: she "shows the way" (*hodigitria*), and is herself "the Sign" of the way, according to the traditional iconography of East and West.

Beginning with Mary's unique cooperation with the working of the Holy Spirit, the Churches developed their prayer to the holy Mother of God, centering it on the person of Christ manifested in his mysteries. In countless hymns and antiphons expressing this prayer, two movements usually alternate with one another: the first "magnifies" the Lord for the "great things" he did for his lowly servant and through her for all human beings (see Luke 1:46–55); the second entrusts the supplications and praises of the children of God to the Mother of Jesus, because she now knows the humanity which,

1. *Lumen Gentium* 62.

in her, the Son of God espoused.

This twofold movement of prayer to Mary has found a privileged expression in the *Ave Maria*:

Hail Mary [or Rejoice, Mary]: the greeting of the angel Gabriel opens this prayer. It is God himself who, through his angel as intermediary, greets Mary. Our prayer dares to take up this greeting to Mary with the regard God had for the lowliness of his humble servant and to exult in the joy he finds in her (see Luke 1:48; Zeph. 3:17b).

Full of grace, the Lord is with thee: These two phrases of the angel's greeting shed light on one another. Mary is full of grace because the Lord is with her. The grace with which she is filled is the presence of him who is the source of all grace. "Rejoice . . . O Daughter of Jerusalem . . . the Lord your God is in your midst" (Zeph. 3:14, 17a). Mary, in whom the Lord himself has just made his dwelling, is the daughter of Zion in person, the ark of the covenant, the place where the glory of the Lord dwells. She is "the dwelling of God . . . with men" (Rev. 21:3). Full of grace, Mary is wholly given over to him who has come to dwell in her and whom she is about to give to the world.

Blessed art thou among women and blessed is the fruit of thy womb, Jesus. After the angel's greeting, we make Elizabeth's greeting our own. "Filled with the Holy Spirit," Elizabeth is the first in the long succession of generations who have called Mary "blessed" (Luke 1:41, 48). "Blessed is she who believed. . . ." (Luke 1:45). Mary is "blessed among women" because she believed in the fulfillment of the Lord's word. Abraham, because of his faith, became a blessing for all the nations of the earth (see Gen. 12:3). Mary, because of her faith, became the mother of believers, through whom all nations of the earth receive him who is God's own blessing: Jesus, the "fruit of thy womb."

Holy Mary, Mother of God: With Elizabeth we marvel, "And why is this granted me, that the mother of my Lord should come to me?" (Luke 1:43). Because she gives us Jesus, her son, Mary is Mother of God and our mother; we can entrust all our cares and petitions to her: she prays for us as she prayed for herself: "Let it be to me according to your word" (Luke 1:38). By entrusting ourselves to her prayer, we abandon ourselves to the will of God together with her: "Thy will be done."

Pray for us sinners, now and at the hour of our death: By asking Mary to pray for us, we acknowledge ourselves to be poor sinners and we address ourselves to the "Mother of Mercy," the All-Holy One. We give ourselves over to her now, in the Today of our lives. And our trust broadens further, already at the present moment, to surrender "the hour of our death" wholly to her care. May she be there as she was at her son's death on the cross. May she welcome us as our mother at the hour of our passing (see John 19:27) to lead us to her son, Jesus, in paradise.

Reflection

G.K. Chesterton

The Well and the Shallows

Men need an image, single, colored, and clear in outline, an image to be called up instantly in the imagination, when what is Catholic is to be distinguished from what claims to be Christian or even what in one sense is Christian. Now I can scarcely remember a time when the image of Our Lady did not stand up in my mind quite definitely, at the mention or the thought of all these things. I was quite distant from these things, and then doubtful about these things; and then disputing with the world for them, and with myself against them; for that is the condition before conversion. But whether the figure was distant, or was dark and mysterious, or was a scandal to my contemporaries, or was a challenge to myself—I never doubted that this figure was the figure of the Faith; that she embodied, as a complete human being still only human, all that this Thing had to say to humanity. The instant I remembered the Catholic Church, I remembered her; when I tried to forget the Catholic Church, I tried to forget her; when I finally saw what was nobler than my fate, the freest and the hardest of all my acts of freedom, it was in front of a gilded and very gaudy little image of her in the port of Brindisi, that I promised the thing that I would do, if I returned to my own land.

Prayer

Pope Francis

Lumen Fidei

Mother, help our faith!

Open our ears to hear God's word and to recognize his voice and call.

Awaken in us a desire to follow in his footsteps, to go forth from our own land and to receive his promise.

Help us to be touched by his love, that we may touch him in faith.

Help us to entrust ourselves fully to him and to believe in his love, especially at times of trial, beneath the shadow of the cross, when our faith is called to mature.

Sow in our faith the joy of the Risen One.

Remind us that those who believe are never alone.

Teach us to see all things with the eyes of Jesus, that he may be light for our path. And may this light of faith always increase in us, until the dawn of that undying day which is Christ himself, your Son, our Lord!

In dangers, in doubts, in difficulties, think of Mary, call upon Mary. Let not her name leave your lips, never suffer it to leave your heart. And that you may more surely obtain the assistance of her prayer, see that you walk in her footsteps. With her for a guide, you will never go astray; while invoking her, you will never lose heart; so long as she is in your mind, you will not be deceived; while she holds your hand, you cannot fall; under her protection, you have nothing to fear; if she walks before you, you will not grow weary; if she shows you favor, you will reach the goal.

—ST. BERNARD OF CLAIRVAUX

Mary at Pentecost

Poem

Pope St. John Paul II
"Embraced by New Time"

My depths are seen into, I am seen through and through.
Open to sight I rise, in that vision gently submerge.
For a long time nobody knew of this;
I told no one the expression of your eyes.

How attentive your stillness: it will always be part of me.
I lift myself toward it, will one day grow so used to it
that I will stand still, transparent as water vanishing
into a dry riverbed—though my body will remain.
Your disciples will come, and hear that my heart beat has stopped.

My life will no longer be weighed deep in my blood,
the road will no longer slip away from my weary feet.
New time now shines in my fading eyes:
it will consume me, and dwell with my heart.
And all shall be full at the last, and left for thought's delight.

I will open out my song and I know its smallest sound,
I will open out my song intent on the whole of your life,
my song possessed by the Event so simple and clear,
which begins in every man, visibly there, yet secret.

In me it was made flesh, was revealed in song with grace,
and came to many, and in them found its own space.

Scripture

Acts 1:13–14, 2:1–4

When they had entered the city, they went to the room upstairs where they were staying, Peter, and John, and James, and Andrew, Philip and Thomas, Bartholomew and Matthew, James son of Alphaeus, and Simon the Zealot, and Judas son of James. All these were constantly devoting themselves to prayer, together with certain women, including Mary the mother of Jesus, as well as his brothers. . . .

When the day of Pentecost had come, they were all together in one place. And suddenly from heaven there came a sound like the rush of a violent wind, and it filled the entire house where they were sitting. Divided tongues, as of fire, appeared among them, and a tongue rested on each of them. All of them were filled with the Holy Spirit and began to speak in other languages, as the Spirit gave them ability.

Reflection

Bishop Barron

Heaven in Stone and Glass

Pentecost is the great feast of the Spirit, the birthday of the Church. And in the Acts of the Apostles, we read that the Virgin Mary was gathered with the Apostles in prayer on Pentecost morning. From the very beginning of the Church's life, Mary has been present—a connection incarnated in the great Gothic cathedrals of Europe.

In the centuries prior to the Gothic period, Christian churches were named for a variety of saints, but from the end of the twelfth and into the thirteenth century, the cathedrals were, almost without exception, named for the Virgin. The great cavernous cathedrals of the Middle Ages were seen, in an almost literal sense, as the body of Mary, places of safety and birth. I can testify that, standing in the midst of Chartres, Amiens, or Notre-Dame de Paris, one feels an overwhelming sense of security, a peacefulness and serenity of spirit. The dark, all-enveloping space is evocative of the womb in which Christ himself was nurtured and in which all members of the Church come to birth.

From the earliest centuries, the Church was referred to as "mother," *mater ecclesiae*, and Mary, the mother of Jesus, was closely associated with it as its symbol, protector, and premier member. Her attitude of acquiescence to God's designs is the safety that is the Church. When the pilgrims came to Chartres, they were hoping to see a most holy relic, the *chemise* (tunic) of the Virgin, but at a deeper level they were seeking security, and it was this spiritual rest that they found in the womb of the cathedral and the embrace of the Virgin. Now, there is nothing easy or cheap about this repose offered by Mary, and they knew it. All over the cathedrals are depictions of the Annunciation, Mary's yes, but there are also vivid reminders of all that flowed from that acceptance: the massacre of the innocents, the flight into Egypt, the awful vigil at the foot of the cross. The peace realized and embodied by Mary is not the peace that the world gives, but rather the serenity beyond pleasure and pain that follows from an acceptance of our role in God's dramatic designs.

The interior space of the church, the body of Notre-Dame, is therefore a place of safety, but it is also, as I suggested above, a womb, a place of gestation and birth. The purpose of the Church is not merely to keep us safe from the dangers of the world; it is to bring us to fullness of life. St. Irenaeus suggested that Adam and Eve in the Garden of Eden were not so much full-fledged adults as adolescents—somewhat unsure of themselves, testing their freedom—and that the whole history of salvation is a long, sometimes tortuous process of development and education, God cajoling his people in the direction of salvation. According to this vision, the Church is that place where the growth, the education, the gestation of the race continues. Our life here below, lived out in the nurturing confines of the Church, is like the development of the fetus in the womb.

Now, to be sure, a womb is a place of safety and comfort, but it is not the proper or final environment for the child. In fact, as the baby grows within her mother, she becomes increasingly uncomfortable, preparing for the moment when she will emerge into the spacious and colorful world for which she is destined. So we gestate in the womb of the mother cathedral, taking in the nourishment of her stories, pictures, and doctrines, and growing, year by year, uncomfortable with this world, readying ourselves for the far richer, broader, and more beautiful world that God is preparing for us. Wombs are secure, but they are not our final home.

Catechism

726

At the end of this mission of the Spirit, Mary became the Woman, the new Eve ("mother of the living"), the mother of the "whole Christ" (see John 19:25–27). As such, she was present with the Twelve, who "with one accord devoted themselves to prayer" (Acts 1:14), at the dawn of the "end time" which the Spirit was to inaugurate on the morning of Pentecost with the manifestation of the Church.

Reflection

Pope St. John Paul II

Redemptoris Mater

Among all believers she is like a "mirror" in which are reflected in the most profound and limpid way "the mighty works of God" (Acts 2:11).

Built by Christ upon the Apostles, the Church became fully aware of these mighty works of God on the day of Pentecost, when those gathered together in the Upper Room "were all filled with the Holy Spirit and began to speak in other tongues, as the Spirit gave them utterance" (Acts 2:4). From that moment there also begins that journey of faith, the Church's pilgrimage through the history of individuals and peoples. We know that at the beginning of this journey Mary is present. We see her in the midst of the Apostles in the Upper Room, "prayerfully imploring the gift of the Spirit."

In a sense her journey of faith is longer. The Holy Spirit had already come down upon her, and she became his faithful spouse at the Annunciation, welcoming the Word of the true God, offering "the full submission of intellect and will . . . and freely assenting to the truth revealed by him," indeed abandoning herself totally to God through "the obedience of faith," whereby she replied to the angel: "Here am I, the servant of the Lord; let it be with me according to your word" (Luke 1:38). The journey of faith made by Mary, whom we see praying in the Upper Room, is thus longer than that of the others gathered there: Mary "goes before them," "leads the way" for them. The moment of Pentecost in Jerusalem had been prepared for by the moment of the Annunciation in Nazareth, as well as by the Cross. In the Upper Room Mary's journey meets the Church's journey of faith.

Prayer

St. Vincent Pallotti

Daily Bread

Immaculate Mother of God, Queen of Apostles, we know that God's commandment of love and our vocation to follow Jesus Christ impels us to cooperate in the mission of the Church. Realizing our own weakness, we entrust the renewal of our personal lives and our apostolate to your intercession.

We are confident that through God's mercy and the infinite merits of Jesus Christ, you, who are our Mother, will obtain the strength of the Holy Spirit as you obtained it for the community of the Apostles gathered in the upper room.

Therefore, relying on your maternal intercession, we are resolved from this moment on to devote our talents, learning, material resources, our health, sickness and trials, and every gift of nature and grace, for the greater glory of God and the salvation of all.

We wish to carry on those activities which especially promote the catholic apostolate for the revival of faith and love of the people of God and so bring all men and women into the faith of Jesus Christ.

And if a time should come when we have nothing more to offer serviceable to this end, we will never cease to pray that there will be one fold and one shepherd, Jesus Christ.

In this way, we hope to enjoy the results of the apostolate of Jesus Christ for all eternity.

Amen.

In the redemptive economy of grace, brought about through the action of the Holy Spirit, there is a unique correspondence between the moment of the Incarnation of the Word and the moment of the birth of the Church. The person who links these two moments is Mary: Mary at Nazareth and Mary in the Upper Room at Jerusalem.

—POPE ST. JOHN PAUL II

Hymn

Ave Regina Caelorum

(Sung from the Feast of the Presentation to the Easter Vigil)

Latin

Ave, Regina caelorum,
ave, Domina angelorum,
salve, radix, salve, porta,
ex qua mundo lux est orta.

Gaude, Virgo gloriosa,
super omnes speciosa;
vale, o valde decora,
et pro nobis Christum exora.

English

Hail, holy Queen of Heavens.
Hail, holy Queen of the Angels.
Hail, Root of Jesse.
Hail, Gate of Heaven.
By you the Light has entered the world.

Rejoice, glorious Virgin,
beautiful among all women.
Hail, radiant Splendor,
intercede with Christ for us.

IV.
Queen *of* Heaven

✷ Mary's Resurrection

Sally Read

Somewhere in the inkwell of that night,
or the shaken clarity of morning
there was a moment that you knew his rising,
and though faith may have led you to expect it,
there's a difference between the shimmering lit
shadow-rings beside a glass of water,
and the drink itself. Where were you, Mother,

when you knew? Did the swords slide cleanly
from your heart? The tight and gritty shadows
of a mother's pain that intimately and silently
mark each step of her child's agony
and graft it deep into her own heart's wall—
did all this fall from you in one gifted
moment, or as you ran to meet him?

Or was there a sudden doubling in you:
the knowledge of God's plan coupling with each
crazed memory—not canceling, but telling
you that each hair of every head is known;
each suffering is dancing with this Love?
See how the pain rises, like vapor from the fields,
its broken scent escaping—you too are lifted.

✷

The Assumption

Poem

Alfred Noyes

"The Assumption—An Answer"

Before earth saw Him she had felt and known
 The small soft feet that thrust like buds in Spring.
The body of Our Lord was all her own.
 Once from the Cross her arms received her King.

Think you that she, who bore Him on her breast,
 Had not the Word still living in her heart?
Or that, because one voice had called her blest
 Her inmost soul had lost the better part?

Henceforth all generations . . . Ah, but that
 You think was but an ancient song she knew!
Millions this night will sing Magnificat,
 And bring at least one strange prediction true.

Think you His Heaven, that deep transcendent state,
 Floats like Murillo's picture in the air?

Or that her life, so heavenly consecrate,
  Had no essential habitation there?

Think you he looked upon her dying face,
  And throned above His burning seraphim,
Felt no especial tenderness or grace
  For her whose life-blood once had throbbed in Him?

Proof of his filial love, His body on earth
  Still lives and breathes, and tells us, night and day,
That earth and Heaven were mingled in His birth
  Through her, who kneels beside us when we pray.

Kneels to the Word made flesh; her living faith
  Kneels to incarnate Love, "not lent but given,"
Assumed to her on earth, and after death
  Assuming her to His own Heart in Heaven.

Scripture

Psalm 132:8

Rise up, O Lord, and go to your resting place,
  you and the ark of your might.

Reflection

Bishop Barron
Catholicism

The fourth Marian dogma, the Assumption of the Virgin, was declared as such by Pope Pius XII in 1950. Before the formal promulgation of the doctrine, Pius sponsored a worldwide survey of the Catholic people, a consultation of the faithful, to see whether they sanctioned this teaching, and the response was overwhelmingly positive. Also, the roots of this dogma in the tradition of the Church are old and deep.

But what precisely does the dogma teach? That Mary, upon leaving this life, was taken, body and soul, into heaven. I fully realize that this assertion can strike the contemporary mind as bizarre, mythological, a holdover from a naïve, prescientific world. First, let us place it within the context of the radically nondualistic perspective of the Bible in regard to the soul and the body. Greek philosophy tends to construe salvation as an escape of the soul from the prison of the body. To see this attitude on full display, consult Plato's dialogue the *Phaedo*, in which Socrates urges his friends not to mourn over his coming death but to see it as a much longed for liberation. This philosophy is utterly alien to the biblical imagination, which does not envision salvation as the separation of the soul from the body, but rather as the transfiguration of the entire self.

To give just two examples of this pervasive attitude, the

authors of both the book of Revelation and the First Letter of Peter dream not of an escape from the world but of a new heavens and a new earth (Rev. 21:1; 2 Pet. 3:13). The dogma of the Assumption of Mary describes the full salvation of this prime disciple of Jesus—Mary's entry, in the fullness of her person, into the presence of God. At the close of the Apostles' Creed, we speak of our hope for "the resurrection of the body." Mary, assumed body and soul into heaven, has experienced precisely this kind of resurrection and hence becomes a sign of hope for the rest of the human race.

If we are to respond adequately to the skeptics, a second observation must be made. When we speak of the Assumption of the Blessed Mother's body, we are not envisioning a journey through space, as though Mary moved up into the sky. The "heavens" are a rich and consistent biblical symbol for the transcendent, for a manner of existence that lies beyond our familiar dimensions of space and time. The Assumption of Mary means that the Blessed Mother was "translated," in the totality of her being, from this dimensional system to the higher one for which we use the symbolically evocative term "heaven."

Perhaps a comparison would help here. Think of a square, a circle, and a triangle plotted out on a two-dimensional plane. Now imagine those figures elevated through the introduction of a third dimension into a cube, a sphere, and a pyramid. They have not so much lost their former identities as found them heightened, deepened, and perfected. What if there were a conscious subject who lived exclusively in a two-dimensional world? He would know only squares, circles, triangles, and so on, and if you spoke to him of cubes, spheres, and pyramids, he would find your language utterly impenetrable, so much nonsense. Heaven is a symbol for a higher dimensional system that contains the dimensions with which we are familiar but that also elevates them and situates them in a richer context. Mary, who exists now in this other world, is not so much *somewhere* else as *somehow* else, and this helps to explain why we can speak of her, especially in her heavenly state, interceding, helping us and praying for us. Again, to people who have known only this world, such a concept will necessarily seem opaque, even ridiculous. The doctrine of Mary's Assumption both whets our appetite for this higher world and teases our minds into the consideration of it.

At this point, I would like to offer just a word of reflection on an idea that is related to the dogma of the Assumption but that is not a formal doctrine of the Church: the teaching concerning the "dormition" or the "falling asleep" of Mary. According to this notion, at the end of her days Mary did not so much die in the ordinary sense but fell asleep in the Lord. Again, although this can strike us as strange, it actually conveys something of great spiritual importance. Death can be taken in a purely biological or physiological sense to mean the cessation of bodily activity: heartbeat, breathing, brain waves, and so on. Or it can be construed in a wider psychological and spiritual sense to mean the full range of feelings, reactions, and fears that accompany this biological dissolution. At the prospect of death, most of us recoil in terror, either at the mystery of it (the unknown is what frightens us the most) or because of the judgment that awaits us. In either case, our horror is prompted by sin, a lack of confident trust in the love of God. What would it be like for a sinless person to approach death? Wouldn't he or she face it with utter calmness of spirit, the way most of us fall effortlessly into the oblivion of sleep each night, convinced that we shall awaken the next morning? That the sinless Mary didn't "die," in the full sense of that term, but merely "fell asleep," confidently expecting a transition into God's dimension, strikes me as a not altogether unreasonable way to speak of the end of Mary's earthly life.

Catechism

966

"Finally the Immaculate Virgin, preserved free from all stain of original sin, when the course of her earthly life was finished, was taken up body and soul into heavenly glory, and exalted by the Lord as Queen over all things, so that she might be the more fully conformed to her Son, the Lord of lords and conqueror of sin and death."[1] The Assumption of the Blessed

1. *Lumen Gentium* 59; see Pius XII, *Munificentissimus Deus* (1950): Denzinger-Schönmetzer 3903; see Rev. 19:16.

Virgin is a singular participation in her Son's Resurrection and an anticipation of the resurrection of other Christians:

> In giving birth you kept your virginity; in your Dormition you did not leave the world, O Mother of God, but were joined to the source of Life. You conceived the living God and, by your prayers, will deliver our souls from death.[2]

Reflection

Fulton Sheen

The World's First Love

In Mary there is a triple transition. In the Annunciation we pass from the holiness of the Old Testament to the holiness of Christ. At Pentecost we pass from the holiness of the historical Christ to the holiness of the Mystical Christ or his Body, which is the Church. . . . The third transition is the Assumption, as she becomes the first human person to realize the historical destiny of the faithful as members of Christ's Mystical Body, beyond time, beyond death, and beyond judgment.

Mary is always in the vanguard of humanity. She is compared to Wisdom, presiding at creation; she is announced as the Woman who will conquer Satan, as the Virgin who will conceive. She becomes the first person since the fall to have a

2. Byzantine Liturgy, *Troparion*, Feast of the Dormition, August 15.

unique and unrepeatable kind of union with God; she mothers the infant Christ in Bethlehem; she mothers the Mystical Christ at Jerusalem; and now, by her Assumption, she goes ahead like her son to prepare a place for us. She participates in the glory of her son, reigns with him, presides at his side over the destinies of the Church in time, and intercedes for us, to him, as he, in his turn, intercedes to the heavenly Father.

Adam came before Eve chronologically. The New Adam, Christ, comes after the New Eve, Mary, chronologically, although existentially he preceded her as the Creator a creature. By stressing for the moment only the time element, Mary always seems to be the advent of what is in store for man. She anticipates Christ for nine months, as she bears heaven within her; she anticipates his Passion at Cana and his Church at Pentecost. Now, in the last great Doctrine of the Assumption, she anticipates heavenly glory, and the definition comes at a time when men think of it least.

Prayer

Pope St. John Paul II

Homily

We exult, O Mary assumed into heaven, as we contemplate you who have been glorified and, in the risen Christ, have become the co-worker of the Holy Spirit in communicating divine life to mankind. In you we see the goal of holiness to which

God calls all the Church's members. In your life we recognize the clear sign of the path to spiritual maturity and Christian holiness. With you and with all the saints we glorify God the Trinity, who sustains our earthly pilgrimage and lives and reigns forever and ever. Amen.

And who, I ask, could believe that the ark of holiness, the dwelling place of the Word of God, the temple of the Holy Spirit, could be reduced to ruin? My soul is filled with horror at the thought that this virginal flesh which had begotten God, had brought him into the world, had nourished and carried him, could have been turned into ashes or given over to be food for worms.

—ST. ROBERT BELLARMINE

A Woman Clothed with the Sun

Poem

St. Thérèse of Lisieux
"Why I Love You, O Mary"

You love us, Mary, as Jesus loves us,
And for us you accept being separated from Him.
To love is to give everything. It's to give oneself.
You wanted to prove this by remaining our support.
The Savior knew your immense tenderness.
He knew the secrets of your maternal heart.
Refuge of sinners, He leaves us to you
When He leaves the Cross to wait for us in Heaven.

Mary, at the top of Calvary standing beside the Cross
To me you seem like a priest at the altar,
Offering your beloved Jesus, the sweet Emmanuel,
To appease the Father's justice . . .
A prophet said, O afflicted Mother,
"There is no sorrow like your sorrow!"
O Queen of Martyrs, while remaining in exile
You lavish on us all the blood of your heart!

Saint John's home becomes your only refuge.
Zebedee's son is to replace Jesus . . .
That is the last detail the Gospel gives.
It tells me nothing more of the Queen of Heaven.
But, O my dear Mother, doesn't its profound silence
Reveal that *The Eternal Word Himself*
Wants to sing the secrets of your life
To charm *your children*, all the Elect of Heaven?

Soon I'll hear that sweet harmony.
Soon I'll go to beautiful Heaven to see you.
You who came *to smile at me* in the morning of my life,
Come smile at me again . . . Mother . . . It's evening now! . . .
I no longer fear the splendor of your supreme glory.
With you I've suffered and now I want
To sing on your lap, Mary, why I love you,
And to go on saying that I am your child! . . .

Scripture

Revelation 12:1–2

A great portent appeared in heaven: a woman clothed with the sun, with the moon under her feet, and on her head a crown of twelve stars. She was pregnant and was crying out in birth pangs, in the agony of giving birth.

Reflection

Bishop Barron
Catholicism

On December 9, 1531, just about ten years after the Spaniards had first brought the faith to Mexico, an Indian man named Juan Diego, a recent convert to Christianity, was making his way along the hill of Tepeyac, just outside the city of Tenochtitlan, which would later evolve into Mexico City. He was heading to morning Mass. He heard a burst of birdsong and turned to see where it was coming from. What he saw took his breath away, for standing before him was a woman clothed in celestial light. The Lady announced herself as the "Mother of the Most High God," and she had a request for Juan Diego: "Would you ask the bishop to construct a temple here in my honor?" Being a simple man, Juan Diego obeyed. He was ushered into the presence of Bishop Juan Zumárraga, a Franciscan friar and a good man, the builder of the first hospital and university in the Americas, and a protector of the native population. Bishop Zumárraga listened patiently to Juan Diego's story, but, understandably enough, he asked Juan Diego for a confirming sign from the heavenly Lady.

On December 12, Juan Diego went once again to Tepeyac and found the Virgin there. She invited him to remove his tilma, the simple, coarse, poncho-like garment he was wearing, and then, with her help, he gathered up a bunch of roses that were, despite the lateness of the year, in bloom. This, she said, would be a sign for the bishop. Juan Diego hurried with his bundle to the bishop's office, but he was made to wait. It is said that officious aides of Zumárraga's tried, without success, to find out what the Indian was carrying in his tilma. Finally, Juan Diego was brought into the bishop's presence. He opened his cloak and the roses spilled out, but then, to Juan Diego's amazement, the bishop and his assistants were kneeling, for on the inside of the tilma was something extraordinary: an image of the woman clothed in light. On the spot, Zumárraga vowed to build the temple the Lady had asked for, and it still stands near the hill of Tepeyac.

One might be tempted to dismiss this as a charming story from a simpler, more credulous time, but the best contradiction to this kind of skepticism is the tilma itself, which is displayed in the massive Basilica of Our Lady of Guadalupe in Mexico City. Careful studies have shown that the tilma is indeed from the sixteenth century and woven from cactus fibers. This juxtaposition is itself puzzling, since that kind of garment, under the best of conditions, usually lasts for, at most, twenty or twenty-five years.

And then there is the image, the strange and beautiful image, which has beguiled millions for the past five hundred years. Scientific analysis has revealed that no known pigmentation was involved and that no underdrawing is discernible. Therefore, just how those colors were transferred onto the tilma is mysterious. Moreover, the symbolic power of the image is extraordinary. The Virgin on the tilma is not a European or an Indian, but a mestiza, a blend of the two races. Mexicans today refer to her affectionately as La Virgen Morena (the brown-skinned Virgin). It is as though the Blessed Mother was humbly identifying herself with the new people who were emerging in that time and place. The cincture that she wears was an Aztec sign of pregnancy, and therefore it is clear that La Virgen Morena is bringing a new life and a new birth to the people of Mexico. She stands in front of the sun, whose rays can be seen behind her, her feet are on the moon, and her mantle is bedecked with stars. The sun, moon, and stars were all deities for the ancient Aztecs, and thus the Lady is declaring herself to be more powerful than the Indian gods. At the same time, she keeps her eyes down and her hands folded in an attitude of prayer, acknowledging that there is one still greater than she.

In recent years, astronomers have noted that the arrangement of the stars on her cloak corresponds precisely to the position of the constellations on December 12, 1531. And perhaps most astonishingly, through microscopic investigation, ophthalmologists have discovered images of human figures in the eye of La Virgen Morena that correspond to the positions such images would have in a functioning eye, and these reflections are credibly of Zumárraga and his confreres at the moment of the unfolding of the tilma. Her name, "Guadalupe," is probably a Spanish deformation of the Nahuatl term *coatlaxopeuh* (pronounced coat-la-soupay), which means "the one who crushes the serpent." This name has a double sense, for the serpent was another chief divinity of the Aztecs, and, in the Christian context, the book of Genesis speaks of the serpent (the tempter) that would strike at the heel of the offspring of the archetypal woman (Gen. 3:15).

Catechism

974–975

The Most Blessed Virgin Mary, when the course of her earthly life was completed, was taken up body and soul into the glory of heaven, where she already shares in the glory of her Son's Resurrection, anticipating the resurrection of all members of his Body.

"We believe that the Holy Mother of God, the new Eve, Mother of the Church, continues in heaven to exercise her maternal role on behalf of the members of Christ" (Paul VI, *Credo of the People of God* 15).

Reflection

St. Thérèse of Lisieux

Story of a Soul

A miracle was necessary for my cure.

A miracle was necessary and it was our Lady of Victories

who worked it. One Sunday during the Novena of Masses, Marie went into the garden, leaving me with Léonie who was reading near the window. After a few moments I began calling in a low tone: "Mama, Mama." Léonie, accustomed to hearing me always calling out like this, didn't pay any attention. This lasted a long time, and then I called her much louder. Marie finally returned. I saw her enter, but I cannot say I recognized her and continued to call her in a louder tone: "Mama." *I was suffering very much* from this forced and inexplicable struggle and Marie was suffering perhaps even more than I. After some futile attempts to show me she was by my side, Marie knelt down near my bed with Léonie and Céline. Turning to the Blessed Virgin and praying with the fervor of a mother begging for the life of her child, *Marie* obtained what she wanted.

Finding no help on earth, poor little Thérèse had also turned toward the Mother of heaven, and prayed with all her heart that she take pity on her. All of a sudden the Blessed Virgin appeared *beautiful* to me, so *beautiful* that never had I seen anything so attractive; her face was suffused with an ineffable benevolence and tenderness, but what penetrated to the very depths of my soul was the "*ravishing smile of the Blessed Virgin*." At that instant, all my pain disappeared, and two large tears glistened on my eyelashes, and flowed down my cheeks silently, but they were tears of unmixed joy. Ah! I thought, the Blessed Virgin smiled at me, how happy I am, but never will I tell anyone for my *happiness would then disappear*.

Without any effort I lowered my eyes, and I saw Marie who was looking down at me lovingly; she seemed moved and appeared to surmise the favor the Blessed Virgin had given me. Ah! it was really to her, to her touching prayers that I owed the grace of the Queen of Heaven's *smile*. Seeing my gaze fixed on the Blessed Virgin, she cried out: "Thérèse is cured!" Yes, the little flower was going to be born again to life, and the luminous *Ray* that had warmed her again was not to stop its favors; the Ray did not act all at once, but sweetly and gently it raised the little flower and strengthened her in such a way that five years later she was expanding on the fertile mountain of Carmel.

Prayer

Akathist Hymn (First Ikos)
Byzantine Traditional

Hail, O you through whom joy will shine forth;
  hail, O you through whom the curse will disappear!
Hail, O Restoration of the fallen Adam;
  hail, O Redemption of the tears of Eve!
Hail, O Peak above the reach of human thought;
  hail, O Depth even beyond the sight of angels!
Hail, O you who have become a kingly throne;
  hail, O you who carries Him who carries all!
Hail, O Star who manifests the Sun;
  hail, O Womb of the divine Incarnation!

Hail, O you through whom creation is renewed;
    hail, O you through whom the Creator becomes a Babe!
Hail, O Bride and Maiden ever-pure!
Amen.

There is never a crack in the ivory tower
Or a hinge to groan in the house of gold
Or a leaf of the rose in the wind to wither
And She grows young as the world grows old.
A Woman clothed with the sun returning
To clothe the sun when the sun is cold.

—G.K. CHESTERTON

The Warrior Queen

Poem

Dante

From *Paradise*

"Virgin Mother, daughter of your Son,
    humbler and loftier past creation's measure,
    the fulcrum of the everlasting plan,
You are she who ennobled human nature
    so highly, that its Maker did not scorn
    to make himself the creature of his creature.
In your womb was the flame of love reborn,
    in the eternal peace of whose warm ray
    this flower has sprung and is so richly grown.
For us you are the torch of the noonday
    of charity; below, you are the spring
    of ever-living hope for men that die.
Lady, so great you are, such strength you bring,
    who does not run to you and looks for grace,
    his wish would seek to fly without a wing.
Not only does your kindness come to brace
    our courage when we beg: often your free
    favor arrives before our prayer's race.

In you is mercy, in you is piety,
in you magnificence, in you the sum
of excellence in all things that come to be."

Scripture

Revelation 12:3–6, 13–17

Then another portent appeared in heaven: a great red dragon, with seven heads and ten horns, and seven diadems on his heads. His tail swept down a third of the stars of heaven and threw them to the earth. Then the dragon stood before the woman who was about to bear a child, so that he might devour her child as soon as it was born. And she gave birth to a son, a male child, who is to rule all the nations with a rod of iron. But her child was snatched away and taken to God and to his throne; and the woman fled into the wilderness, where she has a place prepared by God, so that there she can be nourished for one thousand two hundred sixty days. . . .

So when the dragon saw that he had been thrown down to the earth, he pursued the woman who had given birth to the male child. But the woman was given the two wings of the great eagle, so that she could fly from the serpent into the wilderness, to her place where she is nourished for a time, and times, and half a time. Then from his mouth the serpent poured water like a river after the woman, to sweep her away with the flood. But the earth came to the help of the woman; it opened its mouth and swallowed the river that the dragon had poured from his mouth. Then the dragon was angry with the woman, and went off to make war on the rest of her children, those who keep the commandments of God and hold the testimony of Jesus.

Reflection

Bishop Barron
Homily

Every August 22, the Catholic Church celebrates the Memorial of the Queenship of Mary. I would imagine that most people, upon hearing of this celebration, would think of it as something rather twee and sentimental, a quaint devotion for grandmothers with a taste for saccharine spirituality. But when we examine this feast, as we should, through biblical eyes, a very different picture emerges.

The clearest scriptural indication that Mary of Nazareth is a Queen is a remarkable passage in the twelfth chapter of the book of Revelation. The visionary author sees an extraordinary sign in the sky: a woman clothed with the sun, with the moon at her feet and a coronet of twelve stars on her head. Twelve, of course, is a designation of the tribes of Israel, and the crown is a rather unambiguous indication that we are dealing with a royal figure. It soon becomes clear that this woman is not only a Queen but, more precisely, a Queen mother, for we hear that she is laboring to give birth to a king, one "who is to rule all the nations with a rod of iron" (Rev. 12:5).

And both the Queen mother and the infant King are involved in a terrible struggle. The visionary tells us that a fearsome dragon is poised to devour the baby as soon as it comes forth. But God sweeps up the child and brings him to the safety of the divine throne, while the mother flees to the desert where she finds refuge. In the wake of this, a war breaks out between "Michael and his angels" and the dragon and his angelic supporters (Rev. 12:7). This image is, of course, symbolically rich and multivalent, but at the very least it indicates that the Queen and her kingly son are protagonists in a spiritual warfare of some magnitude. They are, in a word, warriors.

Just before this passage, at the very end of chapter eleven of the book of Revelation (and remember that the chapter designations came many centuries after this text was originally composed), we find the vision of the heavenly temple. Amidst flashes of lightning, peals of thunder, and a mighty hailstorm, the seer spies, within the temple, the ark of the covenant. The ark, we recall, was the container of the remnants of the Ten Commandments, and hence the most sacred object for ancient Israel. Placed within the Holy of Holies in the Jerusalem temple, the ark was understood to be the link between heaven and earth, the definitive bearer of the divine presence. Moreover, at various points throughout its history, Israel brought the ark into battle, most notably when the priests marched with it seven times around the walls of Jericho before those battlements came tumbling down.

This juxtaposition of the vision of the ark in the heavenly temple and the vision of the Queen mother clothed with the sun cannot have been accidental. The author of the book of Revelation is telling us that Mary, the bearer of the Word of God made flesh, was the Ark of the Covenant *par excellence*. And both ark and queen are associated with the spiritual warfare. Like her son, Mary does not fight with the puny weapons of the world, but rather with the weapons of love, forgiveness, compassion, and provocative nonviolence.

Those who have experienced a Jesuit retreat based upon the *Spiritual Exercises* of St. Ignatius will recognize the "two standards" meditation. Ignatius asks the retreatant to imagine a great field of battle. Arrayed on one side, under the standard of the Church, is the army of Christ, and on the other, under the standard of Satan, is the army of the dark powers. Then Ignatius compels the retreatant to make a decision—indeed, the most fundamental and important choice imaginable, the election that will determine everything else he will say and do for the rest of his life: Which army will you join? Bob Dylan posed the same stark spiritual option in his 1979 song "Gotta Serve Somebody": "It may be the devil or it may be the Lord / But you're gonna have to serve somebody." In other areas of life, a fair amount of nuance and subtlety is called for, but at the most basic level, where one determines the fundamental orientation of one's life, things actually become quite simple and clear.

I would suggest that the Memorial of the Queenship of Mary has to do with this choice: Where do you stand in the great spiritual struggle? With whose army do you fight? Do you march under the banner of the Queen mother and her son or with their enemies? Do you go out with the Ark of the Covenant or against it?

Catechism

2853

Victory over the "prince of this world" (John 14:30) was won once for all at the Hour when Jesus freely gave himself up to death to give us his life. This is the judgment of this world, and the prince of this world is "cast out" (John 12:31; Rev. 12:10). "He pursued the woman" (Rev. 12:13–16) but had no hold on her: the new Eve, "full of grace" of the Holy Spirit, is preserved from sin and the corruption of death (the Immaculate Conception and the Assumption of the Most Holy Mother of God, Mary, ever virgin). "Then the dragon was angry with the woman, and went off to make war on the rest of her offspring" (Rev. 12:17). Therefore the Spirit and the Church pray: "Come, Lord Jesus" (Rev. 22:17, 20), since his coming will deliver us from the Evil One.

Reflection

Pope St. John Paul II

Redemptoris Mater

In the salvific design of the Most Holy Trinity, the mystery of the Incarnation constitutes the superabundant fulfillment of the promise made by God to man after original sin, after that first sin whose effects oppress the whole earthly history of man (see Gen. 3:15). And so, there comes into the world a Son, "the seed of the woman" who will crush the evil of sin in its very origins: "he will crush the head of the serpent." As we see from the words of the Protogospel, the victory of the woman's son will not take place without a hard struggle, a struggle that is to extend through the whole of human history. The "enmity," foretold at the beginning, is confirmed in the Apocalypse (the book of the final events of the Church and the world), in which there recurs the sign of the "woman," this time "clothed with the sun" (Rev. 12:1).

Mary, Mother of the Incarnate Word, is placed at the very center of that enmity, that struggle which accompanies the history of humanity on earth and the history of salvation itself. In this central place, she who belongs to the "weak and poor of the Lord" bears in herself, like no other member of the human race, that "glory of grace" which the Father "has bestowed on us in his beloved Son," and this grace determines the extraordinary greatness and beauty of her whole being. Mary thus remains before God, and also before the whole of humanity, as the unchangeable and inviolable sign of God's election, spoken of in Paul's letter: "in Christ . . . he chose us . . . before the foundation of the world, . . . he destined us . . . to be his sons" (Eph. 1:4, 5). This election is more powerful than any experience of evil and sin, than all that "enmity" which marks the history of man. In this history Mary remains a sign of sure hope.

Prayer

St. Alphonsus Liguori

Visits to the Most Holy Sacrament and the Blessed Virgin Mary

My most pure Queen, you are rich in power, and rich in compassion; you are able to and desire to save all. I therefore beseech you, now and always, in the words of the devout Blosius, saying: "O Lady! Protect me in my combats, and confirm me when I am wavering." O most holy Mary, in this great battle in which I am now engaged with hell, always help me; but when you see me wavering and likely to fall, O my Lady, then extend your hand with greater promptitude, and sustain me with greater vigor. O God! How many temptations have I still to overcome before my death! Mary, my hope, my refuge, my strength, protect me, and never allow me to lose the grace of God. And on my part, I resolve always and instantly to have recourse to you in all temptations, saying: Help me, Mary! Mary, help me!

Mary accompanies us, struggles with us, sustains Christians in their fight against the forces of evil. . . . Prayer with Mary, especially the Rosary, has this "suffering" dimension, that is of struggle, a sustaining prayer in the battle against the evil one and his accomplices.

—POPE FRANCIS

Hymn

Regina Caeli

(Sung from the Easter Vigil to Pentecost Sunday)

Latin

Regina caeli, laetare, alleluia,
quia quem meruisti portare, alleluia,
resurrexit sicut dixit, alleluia;
ora pro nobis Deum, alleluia.

Gaude et laetare, Virgo Maria, alleluia.
Quia surrexit Dominus vere, alleluia.

English

Queen of Heaven, rejoice, alleluia.
The Son whom you merited to bear, alleluia,
has risen as he said, alleluia.
Pray for us to God, alleluia.

Rejoice and be glad, O Virgin Mary, alleluia!
For the Lord has truly risen, alleluia.

The Rosary
with Bishop Robert Barron

✵

How to Pray the Rosary

The Rosary prayer actually consists of a series of smaller prayers, all of which take about twenty minutes to pray. In this brief introduction, we will walk through them together; however, all the necessary prayers also appear in each of the four major sections in this guide.

First, you hold the rosary and begin with the sign of the cross:

In the name of the Father, and of the Son, and of the Holy Spirit. Amen.

Next, holding the crucifix of the rosary, you pray the ancient Apostles' Creed, which is a summary of our baptismal promises:

I believe in God,
the Father almighty,
Creator of heaven and earth,
and in Jesus Christ, his only Son, our Lord,
who was conceived by the Holy Spirit,
born of the Virgin Mary,
suffered under Pontius Pilate,

was crucified, died, and was buried;
he descended into hell;
on the third day he rose again from the dead;
he ascended into heaven,
and is seated at the right hand of God the Father almighty;
from there he will come to judge the living and the dead.
I believe in the Holy Spirit,
the holy catholic Church,
the communion of saints,
the forgiveness of sins,
the resurrection of the body,
and life everlasting.
Amen.

Holding the first bead above the crucifix, you then pray the Our Father, which is the prayer that Jesus taught us to pray:

Our Father, who art in heaven,
hallowed be thy name;
thy kingdom come,
thy will be done
on earth as it is in heaven.
Give us this day our daily bread,
and forgive us our trespasses,
as we forgive those who trespass against us;
and lead us not into temptation,

but deliver us from evil.
Amen.

For each of the three beads that follow, you pray the Hail Mary, which is derived, in part, from the greetings of the angel Gabriel and Mary's relative Elizabeth in Scripture (Luke 1:28, 42). (One thing we might pray for during this introductory triplet is an increase in faith, hope, and love.)

Hail Mary, full of grace, the Lord is with thee;
blessed art thou among women,
and blessed is the fruit of thy womb, Jesus.
Holy Mary, Mother of God,
pray for us sinners,
now and at the hour of our death.
Amen.

Next, you pray the Glory Be, which gives praise to the three persons of our one God:

Glory be to the Father, and to the Son, and to the Holy Spirit;
as it was in the beginning, is now, and ever shall be,
world without end.
Amen.

Next, we move into the heart of the Rosary—the five "decades." These are groupings of ten beads separated by an individual bead. Each of these decades corresponds to a "mystery" in the lives of Christ and his mother. When you pray the Rosary, you pray it following one of four categories of mysteries: the Joyful Mysteries, the Sorrowful Mysteries, the Glorious Mysteries, and the Luminous Mysteries. Each of the four major sections of this guide walk you through the Rosary based on one of these sets of mysteries.

The Joyful Mysteries, which are traditionally prayed on Mondays, Saturdays, and, during the season of Advent, on Sundays, are:

1. The Annunciation
2. The Visitation
3. The Nativity
4. The Presentation in the Temple
5. The Finding in the Temple

The Sorrowful Mysteries, which are traditionally prayed on Tuesdays, Fridays, and, during the season of Lent, on Sundays, are:

1. The Agony in the Garden
2. The Scourging at the Pillar
3. The Crowning with Thorns
4. The Carrying of the Cross

5. The Crucifixion and Death

The Glorious Mysteries, which are traditionally prayed on Wednesdays and, outside the seasons of Advent and Lent, on Sundays, are:

1. The Resurrection
2. The Ascension
3. The Descent of the Holy Spirit
4. The Assumption
5. The Coronation of Mary

The Luminous Mysteries, which are traditionally prayed on Thursdays, are:

1. The Baptism of Christ in the Jordan
2. The Wedding Feast at Cana
3. Jesus' Proclamation of the Coming of the Kingdom of God
4. The Transfiguration
5. The Institution of the Eucharist

On the bead before the first decade, you announce the mystery, perhaps followed by a brief reflection or reading from Scripture. (In this guide, I offer two reflection options for each decade: a longer reflection, and, if preferred for public prayer, a shorter reflection.) Next, you pray an Our Father. Then, for each of the ten beads of the decade, you say a Hail Mary, contemplating the first mystery as you pray.

After you pray the tenth Hail Mary, you pray the Glory Be, followed by the prayer requested by the Blessed Virgin Mary in her apparition at Fatima:

> *O my Jesus, forgive us our sins, save us from the fires of hell; lead all souls to heaven, especially those most in need of thy mercy.*

You repeat this cycle of prayers—announcement of the mystery, Our Father, ten Hail Marys, Glory Be, and the Fatima Prayer—for each of the five decades, meditating on the corresponding mystery as you move through each decade.

After completing the five decades, you pray the Hail, Holy Queen:

> *Hail, holy Queen, mother of mercy,*
> *our life, our sweetness, and our hope.*
> *To thee do we cry, poor banished children of Eve;*
> *to thee do we send up our sighs,*
> *mourning and weeping in this valley of tears.*
> *Turn, then, most gracious advocate,*
> *thine eyes of mercy toward us;*
> *and after this, our exile,*
> *show unto us the blessed fruit of thy womb, Jesus.*

O clement, O loving, O sweet Virgin Mary.
Pray for us, O holy Mother of God,
that we may be made worthy of the promises of Christ.

You then recite a concluding prayer:

Let us pray.
O God, whose only begotten Son,
by his life, death, and Resurrection,
has purchased for us the rewards of eternal life,
grant, we beseech thee,
that while meditating on these mysteries
of the most holy Rosary of the Blessed Virgin Mary,
we may imitate what they contain
and obtain what they promise,
through the same Christ our Lord.
Amen.

Finally, you conclude in precisely the same way you started—with the sign of the cross.

The Joyful Mysteries

Opening Prayers

The Sign of the Cross

In the name of the Father, and of the Son, and of the Holy Spirit. Amen.

The Apostles' Creed

I believe in God,
the Father almighty,
Creator of heaven and earth,
and in Jesus Christ, his only Son, our Lord,
who was conceived by the Holy Spirit,
born of the Virgin Mary,
suffered under Pontius Pilate,
was crucified, died, and was buried;
he descended into hell;
on the third day he rose again from the dead;
he ascended into heaven,
and is seated at the right hand of God the Father almighty;
from there he will come to judge the living and the dead.

I believe in the Holy Spirit,
the holy catholic Church,
the communion of saints,
the forgiveness of sins,
the resurrection of the body,
and life everlasting.
Amen.

The Our Father

Our Father, who art in heaven,
hallowed be thy name;
thy kingdom come,
thy will be done
on earth as it is in heaven.
Give us this day our daily bread,
and forgive us our trespasses,
as we forgive those who trespass against us;
and lead us not into temptation,
but deliver us from evil.
Amen.

The Hail Mary (three times)

Hail Mary, full of grace, the Lord is with thee;
blessed art thou among women,
and blessed is the fruit of thy womb, Jesus.

Holy Mary, Mother of God,
pray for us sinners,
now and at the hour of our death.
Amen.

The Glory Be

Glory be to the Father, and to the Son, and to the Holy Spirit;
as it was in the beginning, is now, and ever shall be,
world without end.
Amen.

The First Joyful Mystery: The Annunciation

Reflection

(Long Option)

The Annunciation focuses on the most elevated creature: Mary, the Virgin Mother of God. The angel's greeting to Mary is important: "Hail Mary, full of grace." Mary is being addressed as someone who is able to accept gifts, who is ready to receive. Then the angel announces to the maid of Nazareth that she has been chosen to be the Mother of God. Here is what Gabriel says: "Behold, you will conceive in your womb and bear a son, and you shall name him Jesus. He will be great and will be called Son of the Most High, and the Lord God will give him the throne of David his father, and he will rule over the house of Jacob forever, and of his kingdom there will be no end." No first-century Israelite would have missed the meaning here: this child shall be the fulfillment of the promise made to King David. And this means that the child is, in fact, the King of the world, the one who would bring unity and peace to all the nations. The conviction grew upon Israel that this mysterious descendent of David would be King, not just for a time and not just in an earthly sense, but forever and for all nations. This definitive King of the Jews would be King of the world. He would be our King, as well.

As we pray this decade, let us contemplate how we have allowed Jesus to be the King and Lord over our whole life.

Reflection

(Short Option)

The angel Gabriel announces to Mary that she has been chosen to become the Mother of God. This child, Jesus, would be the fulfillment of the promise made to King David, ruling forever and for all nations.

The Our Father

Our Father, who art in heaven,
hallowed be thy name;
thy kingdom come,
thy will be done
on earth as it is in heaven.
Give us this day our daily bread,
and forgive us our trespasses,
as we forgive those who trespass against us;
and lead us not into temptation,
but deliver us from evil.
Amen.

The Hail Mary (ten times)
Hail Mary, full of grace, the Lord is with thee;
blessed art thou among women,
and blessed is the fruit of thy womb, Jesus.
Holy Mary, Mother of God,
pray for us sinners,
now and at the hour of our death.
Amen.

The Glory Be
Glory be to the Father, and to the Son, and to the Holy Spirit;
as it was in the beginning, is now, and ever shall be,
world without end.
Amen.

The Fatima Prayer
O my Jesus, forgive us our sins, save us from the fires of hell;
lead all souls to heaven, especially those most in need of thy mercy.

✷

The Second Joyful Mystery: The Visitation

Reflection

(Long Option)

Upon hearing the message of Gabriel concerning her own pregnancy and that of her cousin, Mary, we hear, "proceeded in haste into the hill country of Judah" to see Elizabeth.

Why did she go with such speed and purpose? Because she had found her mission, her role in the theo-drama. We are dominated today by the ego-drama in all of its ramifications and implications. The ego-drama is the play that I'm writing, I'm producing, I'm directing, and above all, that I'm starring in. We see this absolutely everywhere in our culture. Freedom of choice reigns supreme: I become the person that I choose to be. But the theo-drama is the great story being told by God, the great play being directed by God. What makes life thrilling is to discover your role in it. This is precisely what has happened to Mary. She has found her role—indeed a climactic role—in the theo-drama, and she wants to commune with Elizabeth, who has also discovered her role in that same drama.

Throughout this decade of the Rosary, let us contemplate what God reveals to us in the mystery of the Visitation. Have we searched for our place in God's story, abandoning the ego-drama for the theo-drama with a response as bold and simple as Mary's?

Reflection

(Short Option)

Upon hearing the message of Gabriel, Mary "proceeded in haste" to see Elizabeth. Why did she go with such speed and purpose? Because she had found her mission, her role in the great story being told by God.

The Our Father

Our Father, who art in heaven,
hallowed be thy name;
thy kingdom come,
thy will be done
on earth as it is in heaven.
Give us this day our daily bread,
and forgive us our trespasses,
as we forgive those who trespass against us;
and lead us not into temptation,
but deliver us from evil.
Amen.

The Hail Mary (ten times)

Hail Mary, full of grace, the Lord is with thee;
blessed art thou among women,
and blessed is the fruit of thy womb, Jesus.
Holy Mary, Mother of God,
pray for us sinners,
now and at the hour of our death.
Amen.

The Glory Be

Glory be to the Father, and to the Son, and to the Holy Spirit;
as it was in the beginning, is now, and ever shall be,
world without end.
Amen.

The Fatima Prayer

O my Jesus, forgive us our sins, save us from the fires of hell;
lead all souls to heaven, especially those most in need of thy mercy.

✴

The Third Joyful Mystery: The Nativity

Reflection

(Long Option)

When we turn to Luke's familiar account of the birth of Jesus, we see that it commences, as one would expect poems and histories in the ancient world to commence, with the invocation of powerful and important people: Emperor Augustus and Quirinius, the governor of Syria. But then Luke pulls the rug out from under us, for we promptly learn that the story isn't about Augustus and Quirinius at all, but rather about two nobodies making their way from one forgotten outpost of Augustus' empire to another. When Mary and Joseph arrived in David's city, there was no room, even at the crude travelers' hostel, and so their child is born in a cave, or as some scholars have recently suggested, the lower level of a dwelling, the humble part of the house where the animals spent the night.

Luke therefore sets up his story as the tale of two rival emperors: Caesar, the king of the world, and Jesus, the baby King. While Caesar rules from his palace in Rome, Jesus has no place to lay his head; while Caesar exercises rangy power, Jesus is wrapped in swaddling clothes; while Caesar surrounds himself with wealthy and sophisticated courtiers, Jesus is surrounded by animals and shepherds of the field. And yet, the baby King is more powerful than Augustus, which is signaled by the presence of an army (*stratias* in the Greek) of angels in the skies over Bethlehem. All four of the Gospels play out as a struggle, culminating in the deadly business of the cross, between the worldly powers and the power of Christ. For Jesus is not simply a kindly prophet with a gentle message of forgiveness; he is God coming in person to assume command. He is the Lord, the Word made flesh.

As we pray this decade, let us contemplate the great mystery of the Nativity and the subversive presentation of the arrival of the new King.

Reflection

(Short Option)

Mary and Joseph arrive in David's city and their child, the Word made flesh, is born in a cave. This is not a sentimental tale but the commencement of a great struggle between the powers of the world and the power of Christ.

The Our Father

Our Father, who art in heaven,
hallowed be thy name;
thy kingdom come,
thy will be done
on earth as it is in heaven.
Give us this day our daily bread,
and forgive us our trespasses,
as we forgive those who trespass against us;
and lead us not into temptation,
but deliver us from evil.
Amen.

The Hail Mary (ten times)

Hail Mary, full of grace, the Lord is with thee;
blessed art thou among women,
and blessed is the fruit of thy womb, Jesus.
Holy Mary, Mother of God,
pray for us sinners,
now and at the hour of our death.
Amen.

The Glory Be

Glory be to the Father, and to the Son, and to the Holy Spirit;
as it was in the beginning, is now, and ever shall be,
world without end.
Amen.

The Fatima Prayer

O my Jesus, forgive us our sins, save us from the fires of hell;
lead all souls to heaven, especially those most in need of thy mercy.

The Fourth Joyful Mystery: The Presentation in the Temple

Reflection

(Long Option)

The importance of this mystery is rooted in the importance of the temple for ancient Israel. The temple was, in practically a literal sense, the dwelling place of the Lord. Of all the mountains in the world, Yahweh preferred Mt. Zion, and here he had chosen to live. It was the place of encounter *par excellence*. At the temple, Israel was most itself and most in touch with its mission to bring the worship of the true God to the whole world. In the temple, divinity and humanity embraced, and the human race was brought back online with God. Whenever someone offered sacrifice in the temple, he was turning his life, his mind, his will back to God. He was becoming "reconciled" (eyelash to eyelash) with the Lord.

But the sins of the nation had, according to the prophet Ezekiel, caused the glory of the Lord to depart from the temple. Therefore, one of the deepest aspirations of Israel's people was to reestablish the temple as the place of right praise so that the glory of the Lord might return. We can hear this longing in the prophets, in the Psalms, and in communities like the Essenes.

When Joseph and Mary bring the infant Jesus into the temple, therefore, we are meant to appreciate that the prophecy of Ezekiel is being fulfilled. The glory of the Lord has returned to his temple.

As we pray this decade, let us contemplate the mystery of the Presentation of the infant Jesus, God with us, here and now.

Reflection

(Short Option)

Joseph and Mary bring the infant Jesus into the temple, the dwelling place of the Lord, fulfilling the prophecy that the glory of Yahweh would return to his temple.

The Our Father

Our Father, who art in heaven,
hallowed be thy name;
thy kingdom come,
thy will be done
on earth as it is in heaven.
Give us this day our daily bread,
and forgive us our trespasses,

as we forgive those who trespass against us;
and lead us not into temptation,
but deliver us from evil.
Amen.

The Hail Mary (ten times)

Hail Mary, full of grace, the Lord is with thee;
blessed art thou among women,
and blessed is the fruit of thy womb, Jesus.
Holy Mary, Mother of God,
pray for us sinners,
now and at the hour of our death.
Amen.

The Glory Be

Glory be to the Father, and to the Son, and to the Holy Spirit;
as it was in the beginning, is now, and ever shall be,
world without end.
Amen.

The Fatima Prayer

O my Jesus, forgive us our sins, save us from the fires of hell;
lead all souls to heaven, especially those most in need of thy mercy.

The Fifth Joyful Mystery: The Finding in the Temple

Reflection

(Long Option)

After their visit to Jerusalem, Mary and Joseph, along with a bevy of their family and friends, were heading home to Nazareth. They presumed that the child Jesus was somewhere among his relatives in the caravan. Instead, he was in the temple of the Lord, conversing with the elders and masters of the Law. Distraught, Mary and Joseph spent three days looking for him. Any parent who has ever searched for a lost child knows the anguish they must have felt. Can you imagine what it was like as they tried to sleep at night, spinning out the worst scenarios in their minds?

When they finally find him, they, with understandable exasperation, upbraid him: "Child, why have you treated us like this? Look, your father and I have been searching for you in great anxiety." But Jesus responds with a kind of devastating laconicism: "Why were you searching for me? Did you not know that I must be in my Father's house?"

The story conveys a truth that runs sharply counter to our sensibilities: even the most powerful familial emotions must, in the end, give way to mission. Though she felt an enormous pull in the opposite direction, Mary let her son go, allowing him to find his.

As we pray the final decade of the Rosary, let us contemplate the paradox at the heart of this joyful mystery: that precisely in the measure that everyone in the family focuses on God's call for one another, the family becomes more loving and peaceful.

Reflection

(Short Option)

After three days looking for him, Mary and Joseph find the young Jesus in the temple. Jesus says, "Did you not know that I must be in my Father's house?"—conveying that familial emotions must give way to mission.

The Our Father

Our Father, who art in heaven,
hallowed be thy name;
thy kingdom come,
thy will be done
on earth as it is in heaven.
Give us this day our daily bread,
and forgive us our trespasses,

as we forgive those who trespass against us;
and lead us not into temptation,
but deliver us from evil.
Amen.

The Hail Mary (ten times)

Hail Mary, full of grace, the Lord is with thee;
blessed art thou among women,
and blessed is the fruit of thy womb, Jesus.
Holy Mary, Mother of God,
pray for us sinners,
now and at the hour of our death.
Amen.

The Glory Be

Glory be to the Father, and to the Son, and to the Holy Spirit;
as it was in the beginning, is now, and ever shall be,
world without end.
Amen.

The Fatima Prayer

O my Jesus, forgive us our sins, save us from the fires of hell;
lead all souls to heaven, especially those most in need of thy mercy.

Closing Prayers

Hail, Holy Queen

Hail, holy Queen, mother of mercy,
our life, our sweetness, and our hope.
To thee do we cry, poor banished children of Eve;
to thee do we send up our sighs,
mourning and weeping in this valley of tears.
Turn, then, most gracious advocate,
thine eyes of mercy toward us;
and after this, our exile,
show unto us the blessed fruit of thy womb, Jesus.
O clement, O loving, O sweet Virgin Mary.
Pray for us, O holy Mother of God,
that we may be made worthy of the promises of Christ.
Amen.

Concluding Prayer

Let us pray.
O God, whose only begotten Son,
by his life, death, and Resurrection,
has purchased for us the rewards of eternal life,
grant, we beseech thee,

that while meditating on these mysteries
of the most holy Rosary of the Blessed Virgin Mary,
we may imitate what they contain
and obtain what they promise,
through the same Christ our Lord.
Amen.

The Sign of the Cross

In the name of the Father, and of the Son, and of the Holy Spirit.
Amen.

The Sorrowful Mysteries

Opening Prayers

The Sign of the Cross

In the name of the Father, and of the Son, and of the Holy Spirit. Amen.

The Apostles' Creed

I believe in God,
the Father almighty,
Creator of heaven and earth,
and in Jesus Christ, his only Son, our Lord,
who was conceived by the Holy Spirit,
born of the Virgin Mary,
suffered under Pontius Pilate,
was crucified, died, and was buried;
he descended into hell;
on the third day he rose again from the dead;
he ascended into heaven,
and is seated at the right hand of God the Father almighty;
from there he will come to judge the living and the dead.

I believe in the Holy Spirit,
the holy catholic Church,
the communion of saints,
the forgiveness of sins,
the resurrection of the body,
and life everlasting.
Amen.

The Our Father

Our Father, who art in heaven,
hallowed be thy name;
thy kingdom come,
thy will be done
on earth as it is in heaven.
Give us this day our daily bread,
and forgive us our trespasses,
as we forgive those who trespass against us;
and lead us not into temptation,
but deliver us from evil.
Amen.

The Hail Mary (three times)

Hail Mary, full of grace, the Lord is with thee;
blessed art thou among women,
and blessed is the fruit of thy womb, Jesus.

Holy Mary, Mother of God,
pray for us sinners,
now and at the hour of our death.
Amen.

The Glory Be

Glory be to the Father, and to the Son, and to the Holy Spirit;
as it was in the beginning, is now, and ever shall be,
world without end.
Amen.

*

The First Sorrowful Mystery: The Agony in the Garden

Reflection

(Long Option)

In the Garden of Gethsemane, the Son of God enters into the psychological and spiritual space of the sinner. Paul the Apostle says that Christ *became* sin. That's his mission: to bring the light and forgiveness of God into the depths of godforsakenness. He's accompanied only by Peter, James, and John, but even those three closest disciples he ultimately leaves behind. He's pressed down to the ground—the great spiritual writers of our tradition interpret this as the sins of the world pressing down upon him—and he sweats blood. Jesus, the very Son of God, enters into the state of alienation from God. He feels the suffering of the lost.

In that state, he offers an anguished prayer: "Father, if you are willing, remove this cup from me." The whole of Jesus' life is a battle against the devil culminating in the cross—and in the garden, the temptation to avoid following God's will is evident.

Yet struggling against every instinct in his body, he demonstrates fortitude, utterly aligning his will to that of the Father: "Yet, not my will but yours be done." Here at the very center of the drama, and from the center of the co-inherence of the divine and human wills, comes this prayer that signals trust in the divine providence.

As we pray this decade, I invite you to see the aching loneliness of Christ in the garden as his entry into the psychological and spiritual space of the sinner, and to see his great prayer in the garden as a guide for our own prayers and the key to lasting joy and peace: "Not my will but yours be done."

Reflection

(Short Option)

Jesus journeys to the Garden of Gethsemane and enters into the alienation and suffering of the spiritual space of sin. In that state, he utterly aligns his will to that of the Father, pointing the way to lasting joy and peace.

The Our Father

Our Father, who art in heaven,
hallowed be thy name;
thy kingdom come,
thy will be done

on earth as it is in heaven.
Give us this day our daily bread,
and forgive us our trespasses,
as we forgive those who trespass against us;
and lead us not into temptation,
but deliver us from evil.
Amen.

The Hail Mary (ten times)

Hail Mary, full of grace, the Lord is with thee;
blessed art thou among women,
and blessed is the fruit of thy womb, Jesus.
Holy Mary, Mother of God,
pray for us sinners,
now and at the hour of our death.
Amen.

The Glory Be

Glory be to the Father, and to the Son, and to the Holy Spirit;
as it was in the beginning, is now, and ever shall be,
world without end.
Amen.

The Fatima Prayer

O my Jesus, forgive us our sins, save us from the fires of hell;
lead all souls to heaven, especially those most in need of thy mercy.

✷

The Second Sorrowful Mystery: The Scourging at the Pillar

Reflection

(Long Option)

After Pilate sentences Jesus to death, he has Jesus scourged at the pillar, which was a customary torture leading up to crucifixion. We know from archeological evidence and from written accounts what this form of punishment was like. Using a variety of weapons and instruments, Roman scourgers would brutalize their victims.

Hans Urs von Balthasar writes that even those passive aspects of Jesus' Passion in which he allows himself to be used—including the scourging at the pillar—are expressions of "his active will to give himself up in self-surrender," a loving completion of God's promise to his people.

Presenting the scourged Jesus to the crowds, Pilate says, "Behold the man." In the delicious irony of John's Gospel, Pilate is unwittingly drawing attention to the fact that Jesus, completely acquiescent to the will of his Father, even to the point of accepting torture and death, is in fact "the man," humanity at its fullest and most free.

Throughout this decade of the Rosary, let us contemplate the brutality endured by Christ during his scourging and see his loving acceptance of suffering as the means through which he conquers sin and redeems humanity.

Reflection

(Short Option)

After Pilate sentences Jesus to crucifixion, he has him scourged at the pillar. Jesus, completely acquiescent to the will of his Father, lovingly accepts his suffering to conquer sin and redeem humanity.

The Our Father

Our Father, who art in heaven,
hallowed be thy name;
thy kingdom come,
thy will be done
on earth as it is in heaven.
Give us this day our daily bread,
and forgive us our trespasses,
as we forgive those who trespass against us;
and lead us not into temptation,
but deliver us from evil.
Amen.

The Hail Mary (ten times)

Hail Mary, full of grace, the Lord is with thee;
blessed art thou among women,
and blessed is the fruit of thy womb, Jesus.
Holy Mary, Mother of God,
pray for us sinners,
now and at the hour of our death.
Amen.

The Glory Be

Glory be to the Father, and to the Son, and to the Holy Spirit;
as it was in the beginning, is now, and ever shall be,
world without end.
Amen.

The Fatima Prayer

O my Jesus, forgive us our sins, save us from the fires of hell;
lead all souls to heaven, especially those most in need of thy mercy.

*

The Third Sorrowful Mystery: The Crowning with Thorns

Reflection

(Long Option)

Upon being presented to Pilate, Jesus is asked: "Are you the King of the Jews?" A blandly affirmative answer comes: "You say so." This leads the Roman soldiers to place a purple military cloak on his shoulders, a reed in his right hand, and a crown of thorns on his head. They say, "Hail, King of the Jews," and they further mock him by kneeling before him, spitting on him, and striking him on the head with the reed.

But Mark's Gospel does not want us to miss the irony that, precisely as the King of the Jews and the Son of David, Jesus is implicitly King to those soldiers, for the mission of the Davidic king is the unification not only of the tribes of Israel but also of the tribes of all the world. In a meditation he wrote on this mystery, Fulton Sheen calls this mockery of the true King by the soldiers—who presume Jesus' kingship to be false—an atonement for the "sins of the mind," such as egotism, doubt, and pride. The key to honor in the kingdom of God is the willingness to suffer out of love, to give one's life away as a gift. Look at the lives of the saints. It is never about aggrandizing the ego, but rather emptying it out.

For this decade, let us savor the way that Christ absorbs the mockery and hatred of the crowd, and thereby reveals the quality of the divine forgiveness and love.

Reflection

(Short Option)

The Roman soldiers mockingly put a crown of thorns on the head of Jesus. The true King absorbs the mockery and hatred of the crowd, and thereby reveals the quality of the divine forgiveness and love.

The Our Father

Our Father, who art in heaven,
hallowed be thy name;
thy kingdom come,
thy will be done
on earth as it is in heaven.
Give us this day our daily bread,
and forgive us our trespasses,
as we forgive those who trespass against us;
and lead us not into temptation,
but deliver us from evil.
Amen.

The Hail Mary (ten times)

Hail Mary, full of grace, the Lord is with thee;
blessed art thou among women,
and blessed is the fruit of thy womb, Jesus.
Holy Mary, Mother of God,
pray for us sinners,
now and at the hour of our death.
Amen.

The Glory Be

Glory be to the Father, and to the Son, and to the Holy Spirit;
as it was in the beginning, is now, and ever shall be,
world without end.
Amen.

The Fatima Prayer

O my Jesus, forgive us our sins, save us from the fires of hell;
lead all souls to heaven, especially those most in need of thy mercy.

The Fourth Sorrowful Mystery: The Carrying of the Cross

Reflection

(Long Option)

Carrying the cross must become the very structure of the Christian life. Jesus said, "Whoever does not take up his cross and follow after me is not worthy of me." This saying must have been gut-wrenching to his first-century audience, for they knew what the cross meant. It meant a death in utter agony, nakedness, and humiliation. They didn't think of the cross automatically in religious terms, as we do, for they knew it in all of its awful power. Yet Jesus places this terrible image at the very center of the spiritual life.

How should we take up our own cross? We do so by being willing to suffer as Jesus did. We carry our cross in imitation of Christ—loving what he loved, despising what he despised. If God is willing to break open his own heart, then we must be willing to break open our hearts for others. Jesus bore the burdens of the whole world, and this is what we must do—actively, proactively, seeking out ways to lighten other people's loads.

As we pray this decade of the Rosary, let us contemplate the centrality of this journey of self-sacrifice in the Christian life.

Reflection

(Short Option)

After being scourged and crowned with thorns, Jesus is made to carry his cross. Jesus places this terrible image at the very center of the spiritual life, and we take up our own cross by being willing to suffer as Jesus did.

The Our Father

Our Father, who art in heaven,
hallowed be thy name;
thy kingdom come,
thy will be done
on earth as it is in heaven.
Give us this day our daily bread,
and forgive us our trespasses,
as we forgive those who trespass against us;
and lead us not into temptation,
but deliver us from evil.
Amen.

The Hail Mary (ten times)
Hail Mary, full of grace, the Lord is with thee;
blessed art thou among women,
and blessed is the fruit of thy womb, Jesus.
Holy Mary, Mother of God,
pray for us sinners,
now and at the hour of our death.
Amen.

The Glory Be
Glory be to the Father, and to the Son, and to the Holy Spirit;
as it was in the beginning, is now, and ever shall be,
world without end.
Amen.

The Fatima Prayer
O my Jesus, forgive us our sins, save us from the fires of hell;
lead all souls to heaven, especially those most in need of thy mercy.

The Fifth Sorrowful Mystery: The Crucifixion and Death

Reflection

(Long Option)

Christians have become so accustomed to seeing the crucifix—in churches, in schools, on seasonal greeting cards, or worn as jewelry around people's necks—that they have lost any sense of how awful and strange it is. But to the first Christians, the cross of Christ was that and more. Paul called it "a stumbling block to the Jews and foolishness to Gentiles," insinuating that it was sure to bother just about everybody. For the first several centuries of Christianity, artists were reluctant to depict the death of the Lord because it was just too terrible. And yet, Paul can say, "We proclaim Christ crucified," and the entire Christian tradition—from Augustine to Francis of Assisi to Dante to Ignatius of Loyola to Trappist monks in the hills of Kentucky—has echoed him. Somehow they knew that writhing figure pinned to his cross *is* the whole story.

What is that story? The Crucifixion of Jesus is God's judgment on the world and the fullest expression of the divine anger at sin. We are meant to see on that cross not simply a violent display, but rather our own ugliness. What brought Jesus to the cross? Stupidity, anger, mistrust, institutional injustice, betrayal of friends, denial, unspeakable cruelty, scapegoating, and fear. In other words, all of our dysfunction is revealed on that cross. In the light of the cross, no one can honestly say, "I'm okay, and you're okay." In the tormented face of Christ crucified, we know that something has gone terribly wrong with God's creation, that we are like prisoners chained inside of an escape-proof prison, that we are at war with ourselves.

Does this mean God the Father is a cruel taskmaster demanding a bloody sacrifice to appease his anger? No, because we also see something else in the brutality of the cross. We see that God himself has come to stand with us—shoulder to shoulder—in our dysfunction. Jesus' Crucifixion was the opening up of the divine heart so that we could see that no sin of ours could finally separate us from the love of God.

As we pray this final decade, let us savor the strange beauty and the mystery of the crucified Son of God.

Reflection

(Short Option)

Jesus is brutally crucified. This Crucifixion is the fullest expression of the divine anger at sin. But it is also the opening up of the divine heart so that we could see that no sin of ours could finally separate us from God's love.

The Our Father

Our Father, who art in heaven,
hallowed be thy name;
thy kingdom come,
thy will be done
on earth as it is in heaven.
Give us this day our daily bread,
and forgive us our trespasses,
as we forgive those who trespass against us;
and lead us not into temptation,
but deliver us from evil.
Amen.

The Hail Mary (ten times)

Hail Mary, full of grace, the Lord is with thee;
blessed art thou among women,
and blessed is the fruit of thy womb, Jesus.
Holy Mary, Mother of God,
pray for us sinners,
now and at the hour of our death.
Amen.

The Glory Be

Glory be to the Father, and to the Son, and to the Holy Spirit;
as it was in the beginning, is now, and ever shall be,
world without end.
Amen.

The Fatima Prayer

O my Jesus, forgive us our sins, save us from the fires of hell;
lead all souls to heaven, especially those most in need of thy mercy.

Closing Prayers

Hail, Holy Queen

Hail, holy Queen, mother of mercy,
our life, our sweetness, and our hope.
To thee do we cry, poor banished children of Eve;
to thee do we send up our sighs,
mourning and weeping in this valley of tears.
Turn, then, most gracious advocate,
thine eyes of mercy toward us;
and after this, our exile,
show unto us the blessed fruit of thy womb, Jesus.
O clement, O loving, O sweet Virgin Mary.
Pray for us, O holy Mother of God,
that we may be made worthy of the promises of Christ.
Amen.

Concluding Prayer

Let us pray.
O God, whose only begotten Son,
by his life, death, and Resurrection,
has purchased for us the rewards of eternal life,
grant, we beseech thee,

that while meditating on these mysteries
of the most holy Rosary of the Blessed Virgin Mary,
we may imitate what they contain
and obtain what they promise,
through the same Christ our Lord.
Amen.

The Sign of the Cross

In the name of the Father, and of the Son, and of the Holy Spirit.
Amen.

The Glorious Mysteries

Opening Prayers

The Sign of the Cross

In the name of the Father, and of the Son, and of the Holy Spirit. Amen.

The Apostles' Creed

I believe in God,
the Father almighty,
Creator of heaven and earth,
and in Jesus Christ, his only Son, our Lord,
who was conceived by the Holy Spirit,
born of the Virgin Mary,
suffered under Pontius Pilate,
was crucified, died, and was buried;
he descended into hell;
on the third day he rose again from the dead;
he ascended into heaven,
and is seated at the right hand of God the Father almighty;
from there he will come to judge the living and the dead.

I believe in the Holy Spirit,
the holy catholic Church,
the communion of saints,
the forgiveness of sins,
the resurrection of the body,
and life everlasting.
Amen.

The Our Father

Our Father, who art in heaven,
hallowed be thy name;
thy kingdom come,
thy will be done
on earth as it is in heaven.
Give us this day our daily bread,
and forgive us our trespasses,
as we forgive those who trespass against us;
and lead us not into temptation,
but deliver us from evil.
Amen.

The Hail Mary (three times)

Hail Mary, full of grace, the Lord is with thee;
blessed art thou among women,
and blessed is the fruit of thy womb, Jesus.

Holy Mary, Mother of God,
pray for us sinners,
now and at the hour of our death.
Amen.

The Glory Be

Glory be to the Father, and to the Son, and to the Holy Spirit;
as it was in the beginning, is now, and ever shall be,
world without end.
Amen.

✶

The First Glorious Mystery: The Resurrection

Reflection

(Long Option)

In John's magnificent account of the Resurrection, he says that it was early in the morning on the first day of the week. It was still dark—just the way it was at the beginning of time before God said, "Let there be light." But a light was about to shine, and a new creation was about to appear.

The stone had been rolled away. That stone, blocking the entrance to the tomb of Jesus after his Passion and Crucifixion, stands for the finality of death. When someone that we love dies, it is as though a great stone is rolled across them, permanently blocking our access to them. And this is why we weep at death—not just in grief but in a kind of existential frustration.

But for Jesus, the stone had been rolled away. What was dreamed about, what endured as a hope against hope, has become a reality. God has opened the grave of his Son, and the bonds of death have been shattered forever. The Resurrection is the clearest indication of the lordship of Jesus.

The Resurrection reveals certain definite truths. First, that Jesus, having gone all the way down, having journeyed into pain, despair, alienation, death itself, to the limits of godforsakenness, now includes in the divine mercy all those who had wandered far from God. No matter how far we run from the Father, we are always running toward the outstretched arms of the Son.

A second truth is that, in our conflicted world, Christ is not on the side of the scapegoaters but rather on the side of the scapegoated victim. The true God does not sanction a community created through violence; rather, he sanctions what Jesus called the kingdom of God, a society grounded in forgiveness, love, and redemption.

So awed were the disciples by Jesus' victory over death and sin and scapegoating in the Resurrection—and you can sense it in every book and letter of the New Testament—that they awaited the imminent arrival of the new state of affairs, the return of Jesus and the establishment of God's kingdom. The old world was over, broken, compromised, its destruction now just a matter of time.

As we pray this first decade, let us contemplate how much Christ loves us and how his love changes the world.

Reflection

(Short Option)

Jesus the Lord is raised from the dead, revealing that he has gone to the limits of godforsakenness to reach sinners; that he is on the side of the scapegoated victim; and that the destruction of the old world is just a matter of time.

The Our Father

Our Father, who art in heaven,
hallowed be thy name;
thy kingdom come,
thy will be done
on earth as it is in heaven.
Give us this day our daily bread,
and forgive us our trespasses,
as we forgive those who trespass against us;
and lead us not into temptation,
but deliver us from evil.
Amen.

The Hail Mary (ten times)

Hail Mary, full of grace, the Lord is with thee;
blessed art thou among women,
and blessed is the fruit of thy womb, Jesus.

Holy Mary, Mother of God,
pray for us sinners,
now and at the hour of our death.
Amen.

The Glory Be

Glory be to the Father, and to the Son, and to the Holy Spirit;
as it was in the beginning, is now, and ever shall be,
world without end.
Amen.

The Fatima Prayer

O my Jesus, forgive us our sins, save us from the fires of hell;
lead all souls to heaven, especially those most in need of thy mercy.

The Second Glorious Mystery: The Ascension

Reflection

(Long Option)

After commissioning his disciples—and us—to proclaim the Gospel to the whole world, Jesus ascends to heaven, where he takes his place at God's right hand.

How can we even begin to make sense of this mystery, and what does it have to do with us? When we consider the Ascension, it's important to understand that Jesus has not gone up, up, and away, but rather, if I can put it this way, more deeply into our world. He has gone to a dimension that transcends and yet impinges upon our universe. And the prayer of Jesus is that the earth will be filled with the glory of God, that it will be transformed and elevated according to God's purposes. As Jesus leaves the scene—at least in the most obvious sense—he opens the stage for us, so that we might act in his name and in accord with his Spirit. It is precisely those who are most focused on the things of heaven that do most good here below.

Those who pray most intently are most effective in the practical realm. This is opened up by the Ascension.

For this decade, meditate on the great mystery of Jesus' bodily Ascension, which is an invitation for us to go on mission.

Reflection

(Short Option)

After commissioning his disciples to proclaim the Gospel to the world, Jesus ascends to heaven, simultaneously going more deeply into our world and opening the stage for us to act in his name and in accord with his Spirit.

The Our Father

Our Father, who art in heaven,
hallowed be thy name;
thy kingdom come,
thy will be done
on earth as it is in heaven.
Give us this day our daily bread,
and forgive us our trespasses,
as we forgive those who trespass against us;
and lead us not into temptation,
but deliver us from evil.
Amen.

The Hail Mary (ten times)
Hail Mary, full of grace, the Lord is with thee;
blessed art thou among women,
and blessed is the fruit of thy womb, Jesus.
Holy Mary, Mother of God,
pray for us sinners,
now and at the hour of our death.
Amen.

The Glory Be
Glory be to the Father, and to the Son, and to the Holy Spirit;
as it was in the beginning, is now, and ever shall be,
world without end.
Amen.

The Fatima Prayer
O my Jesus, forgive us our sins, save us from the fires of hell;
lead all souls to heaven, especially those most in need of thy mercy.

The Third Glorious Mystery: The Descent of the Holy Spirit

Reflection

(Long Option)

After Jesus' Ascension, the disciples—the core of the Church—are gathered in the upper room, where the Holy Spirit descends upon them. The Spirit is not a force or a principle, but rather a person, that divine person who is the love shared by the Father and the Son, the love that God is. From that event, timorous and largely uneducated men became fearless evangelists, ready and able to spread the Gospel far and wide.

We get some clues as to the nature of the Holy Spirit from the descriptions offered in the New Testament: wind and flame. The term "Holy Spirit," of course, just means Holy Breath—*Spiritus Sanctus*. Wind is mysterious, blowing where it will, coming and going in unpredictable ways. When you have the Holy Spirit in your life, you are not in control. You cannot command the Spirit to come; you have to wait for him and pray for him, as the disciples are portrayed as doing. And once he arrives, you have to be ready to move according to his prompting.

And the Spirit is like fire. And mind you, not just fire, but tongues of fire. The Holy Spirit, who *is* nothing but communication between the Father and the Son, inspires fiery speech: clear, distinct, and uncompromising speech on behalf of Jesus. And this proclamation is public, not private. The first thing the disciples do once they realize that the fire has fallen upon them is to go out and preach the Gospel.

As we pray this decade of the Rosary, let us contemplate the importance of this mystery for the life of the Church today and ponder our mission to continue boldly and publicly to witness to Jesus Christ.

Reflection

(Short Option)

After Jesus' Ascension, the disciples are gathered in the upper room, where the Holy Spirit descends upon them, its wind and flames sending them—and us—on a mission of bold and public evangelization.

The Our Father

Our Father, who art in heaven,
hallowed be thy name;
thy kingdom come,
thy will be done
on earth as it is in heaven.

Give us this day our daily bread,
and forgive us our trespasses,
as we forgive those who trespass against us;
and lead us not into temptation,
but deliver us from evil.
Amen.

The Hail Mary (ten times)
Hail Mary, full of grace, the Lord is with thee;
blessed art thou among women,
and blessed is the fruit of thy womb, Jesus.
Holy Mary, Mother of God,
pray for us sinners,
now and at the hour of our death.
Amen.

The Glory Be
Glory be to the Father, and to the Son, and to the Holy Spirit;
as it was in the beginning, is now, and ever shall be,
world without end.
Amen.

The Fatima Prayer
O my Jesus, forgive us our sins, save us from the fires of hell;
lead all souls to heaven, especially those most in need of thy mercy.

✷

The Fourth Glorious Mystery: The Assumption

Reflection

(Long Option)

The *Catechism of the Catholic Church*, quoting *Lumen Gentium*, teaches that "the Immaculate Virgin, preserved free from all stain of original sin, when the course of her earthly life was finished, was taken up body and soul into heavenly glory." In other words, Mary is the first participant in the fullness of Christ's Resurrection.

In her great Magnificat, Mary is the new Isaiah, the new Jeremiah, the new Ezekiel, for she announces with greatest clarity and joy the coming of the Messiah. What was only vaguely foreseen in those great prophetic figures is now in clear focus: "He has shown the strength of his arm; he has scattered the proud in their conceit. . . . He has filled the hungry with good things and the rich he has sent away empty. He has come to the help of his servant Israel, for he has remembered his promise of mercy, the promise he made to our fathers, to Abraham and his children forever." There is nothing stronger or more beautiful in any of the prophets.

But Mary is more than strong and beautiful; she is the sinless one, the perfect disciple. Mary, who exists now in this other world, is not so much *somewhere* else as *somehow* else, and this helps to explain why we can speak of her, especially in her heavenly state, as interceding and praying for us.

For this decade, let us contemplate Mary's critical role in salvation history, culminating in her bodily Assumption, which, like the Ascension of Jesus, draws us toward a higher world.

Reflection

(Short Option)

As the sinless one and the perfect disciple, Mary is assumed—body and soul—into the dimension of God. She is not so much *somewhere* else as *somehow* else, and intercedes and prays for us in her heavenly state.

The Our Father

Our Father, who art in heaven,
hallowed be thy name;
thy kingdom come,
thy will be done
on earth as it is in heaven.
Give us this day our daily bread,
and forgive us our trespasses,

as we forgive those who trespass against us;
and lead us not into temptation,
but deliver us from evil.
Amen.

The Hail Mary (ten times)

Hail Mary, full of grace, the Lord is with thee;
blessed art thou among women,
and blessed is the fruit of thy womb, Jesus.
Holy Mary, Mother of God,
pray for us sinners,
now and at the hour of our death.
Amen.

The Glory Be

Glory be to the Father, and to the Son, and to the Holy Spirit;
as it was in the beginning, is now, and ever shall be,
world without end.
Amen.

The Fatima Prayer

O my Jesus, forgive us our sins, save us from the fires of hell;
lead all souls to heaven, especially those most in need of thy mercy.

✴

The Fifth Glorious Mystery: The Coronation of Mary

Reflection

(Long Option)

The *Catechism* also teaches us that Mary, having been assumed body and soul into heaven, is "exalted by the Lord as Queen over all things, so that she might be more fully conformed to her Son, the Lord of lords and conqueror of sin and death."

The Queenship of Mary, however, is far from a sentimental image. One of the great biblical points of reference for the coronation of Mary is the twelfth chapter of the book of Revelation. John the visionary sees "a great portent" in heaven: "a woman clothed with the sun, with the moon under her feet, and on her head a crown of twelve stars." Clothed with the sun and with the moon under her feet, she is a figure of cosmic significance and power; and crowned, coronated, we know that she is a Queen.

Then we discover that she is a Queen mother, for she was "crying out in birth pangs, in the agony of giving birth." Next, we learn that this cosmic Queen mother is also a warrior:

"Another portent appeared in heaven; a great red dragon, with seven heads and ten horns. . . . The dragon stood before the woman who was about to bear a child, so that he might devour her child as soon as it was born." What does the red dragon symbolize? Rooted in references from Psalm 89, from the prophet Isaiah, and from the book of Genesis, the red dragon is a sort of summation of all of the forces that stand opposed to God and God's creative intention for the human race. He stands athwart the woman and her son.

After the woman's child is born, the son is snatched away, and then a great war breaks out in heaven—Michael and his angels against the dragon and his angels—and the enemy is thrown down. What is being portrayed here, in beautifully vivid language, is the fact that the Queen of Heaven and her son are the victors in a great cosmic struggle. They embody the victory of God over the forces of chaos, violence, hatred, cruelty, oppression, and injustice.

As we pray this last decade, contemplate the coronation of Mary in heaven—not as a sentimental ceremony, but as a dramatic and subversive mystery, the total victory of God in Christ.

Reflection

(Short Option)

After being assumed body and soul into heaven, Mary is crowned by the Lord as Queen over all things. This is not a sentimental ceremony but a dramatic and subversive mystery, the total victory of God in Christ.

The Our Father

Our Father, who art in heaven,
hallowed be thy name;
thy kingdom come,
thy will be done
on earth as it is in heaven.
Give us this day our daily bread,
and forgive us our trespasses,
as we forgive those who trespass against us;
and lead us not into temptation,
but deliver us from evil.
Amen.

The Hail Mary (ten times)

Hail Mary, full of grace, the Lord is with thee;
blessed art thou among women,
and blessed is the fruit of thy womb, Jesus.
Holy Mary, Mother of God,
pray for us sinners,
now and at the hour of our death.
Amen.

The Glory Be

Glory be to the Father, and to the Son, and to the Holy Spirit;
as it was in the beginning, is now, and ever shall be,
world without end.
Amen.

The Fatima Prayer

O my Jesus, forgive us our sins, save us from the fires of hell;
lead all souls to heaven, especially those most in need of thy mercy.

Closing Prayers

Hail, Holy Queen

Hail, holy Queen, mother of mercy,
our life, our sweetness, and our hope.
To thee do we cry, poor banished children of Eve;
to thee do we send up our sighs,
mourning and weeping in this valley of tears.
Turn, then, most gracious advocate,
thine eyes of mercy toward us;
and after this, our exile,
show unto us the blessed fruit of thy womb, Jesus.
O clement, O loving, O sweet Virgin Mary.
Pray for us, O holy Mother of God,
that we may be made worthy of the promises of Christ.
Amen.

Concluding Prayer

Let us pray.
O God, whose only begotten Son,
by his life, death, and Resurrection,
has purchased for us the rewards of eternal life,
grant, we beseech thee,

that while meditating on these mysteries
of the most holy Rosary of the Blessed Virgin Mary,
we may imitate what they contain
and obtain what they promise,
through the same Christ our Lord.
Amen.

The Sign of the Cross

In the name of the Father, and of the Son, and of the Holy Spirit.
Amen.

The Luminous Mysteries

Opening Prayers

The Sign of the Cross

In the name of the Father, and of the Son, and of the Holy Spirit. Amen.

The Apostles' Creed

I believe in God,
the Father almighty,
Creator of heaven and earth,
and in Jesus Christ, his only Son, our Lord,
who was conceived by the Holy Spirit,
born of the Virgin Mary,
suffered under Pontius Pilate,
was crucified, died, and was buried;
he descended into hell;
on the third day he rose again from the dead;
he ascended into heaven,
and is seated at the right hand of God the Father almighty;
from there he will come to judge the living and the dead.

I believe in the Holy Spirit,
the holy catholic Church,
the communion of saints,
the forgiveness of sins,
the resurrection of the body,
and life everlasting.
Amen.

The Our Father

Our Father, who art in heaven,
hallowed be thy name;
thy kingdom come,
thy will be done
on earth as it is in heaven.
Give us this day our daily bread,
and forgive us our trespasses,
as we forgive those who trespass against us;
and lead us not into temptation,
but deliver us from evil.
Amen.

The Hail Mary (three times)

Hail Mary, full of grace, the Lord is with thee;
blessed art thou among women,
and blessed is the fruit of thy womb, Jesus.
Holy Mary, Mother of God,
pray for us sinners,
now and at the hour of our death.
Amen.

The Glory Be

Glory be to the Father, and to the Son, and to the Holy Spirit;
as it was in the beginning, is now, and ever shall be,
world without end.
Amen.

✦

The First Luminous Mystery: The Baptism of Christ in the Jordan

Reflection

(Long Option)

How strange and scandalous seems the baptism of Jesus. Christ the Lord, the Messiah, the Son of God, the sinless Lamb who takes away the sins of the world, receives for himself the baptism of John, a baptism of repentance. Why is Jesus seeking a baptism of repentance? The difficulty is reflected in the Baptist's confusion: "I should be baptized by you; and yet you come to me." It cannot be true that the Lord Jesus is a sinner, because if this is true, all of Christian revelation is undermined.

As is usually the case with the Bible, what we have here is a startling surprise. Before ever a word passes Jesus' lips, he is presenting his mission. In this gesture, God lays aside his glory and humbly joins us in the muddy waters of our sinfulness. Though sinless, Christ stands with us. Though we are sinners, Christ does not remain aloof. Jesus says, "Give in for now. We must do this to fulfill all righteousness." Fulfilling righteousness, in the old dispensation, would have meant something like "doing what God wants," or "getting right with God." Yet God in Christ takes this a step further. Now we see that "all righteousness" has to do with God's setting things right with us and for us by humbly standing with the sinners he means to save.

As we pray this first decade, let us contemplate our own Baptism, which unites us to the Lamb of God, who takes away the sins of the world.

Reflection

(Short Option)

Jesus, the sinless Lamb of God, comes to receive a baptism of repentance from John. In this stunning gesture, God humbly joins us in the muddy waters of our sinfulness.

The Our Father

Our Father, who art in heaven,
hallowed be thy name;
thy kingdom come,
thy will be done
on earth as it is in heaven.
Give us this day our daily bread,
and forgive us our trespasses,
as we forgive those who trespass against us;

and lead us not into temptation,
but deliver us from evil.
Amen.

The Hail Mary (ten times)

Hail Mary, full of grace, the Lord is with thee;
blessed art thou among women,
and blessed is the fruit of thy womb, Jesus.
Holy Mary, Mother of God,
pray for us sinners,
now and at the hour of our death.
Amen.

The Glory Be

Glory be to the Father, and to the Son, and to the Holy Spirit;
as it was in the beginning, is now, and ever shall be,
world without end.
Amen.

The Fatima Prayer

O my Jesus, forgive us our sins, save us from the fires of hell;
lead all souls to heaven, especially those most in need of thy mercy.

The Second Luminous Mystery: The Wedding Feast at Cana

Reflection

(Long Option)

Weddings are a consistent biblical symbol for the mystical union between God and his people. God wants to marry his people Israel because he loves them so passionately. He wants to fill them with his own life, consummating the marriage, if you will. Now, what is the fulfillment of this prophecy? Nothing other than the Incarnation, when a divine nature and a human nature came together in the unity of a divine person to form a marriage between God and Israel. Jesus is the wedding of heaven and earth, the marriage of divinity and humanity; he is the Bridegroom and the Church is the Bride. In him, the most intimate union is achieved between God and the world.

At this wedding, Jesus changes 180 gallons of water into the wine of the divine life—an intoxication of grace! When we are infused with the divine life, when we are married to God, life never runs out.

For this decade, let us consider the great mystery of Christ's own wedding feast, the abundance of divine grace coming to Israel and all of humanity through the Incarnation.

Reflection

(Short Option)

At the wedding feast at Cana, Jesus changes 180 gallons of water into the wine of the divine life—an intoxication of grace! When we are infused with the divine life, when we are married to God, life never runs out.

The Our Father

Our Father, who art in heaven,
hallowed be thy name;
thy kingdom come,
thy will be done
on earth as it is in heaven.
Give us this day our daily bread,
and forgive us our trespasses,
as we forgive those who trespass against us;
and lead us not into temptation,
but deliver us from evil.
Amen.

The Hail Mary (ten times)

Hail Mary, full of grace, the Lord is with thee;
blessed art thou among women,
and blessed is the fruit of thy womb, Jesus.
Holy Mary, Mother of God,
pray for us sinners,
now and at the hour of our death.
Amen.

The Glory Be

Glory be to the Father, and to the Son, and to the Holy Spirit;
as it was in the beginning, is now, and ever shall be,
world without end.
Amen.

The Fatima Prayer

O my Jesus, forgive us our sins, save us from the fires of hell;
lead all souls to heaven, especially those most in need of thy mercy.

✵

The Third Luminous Mystery: Jesus' Proclamation of the Coming of the Kingdom of God

Reflection

(Long Option)

The first words out of the mouth of Jesus in the Gospel of Mark are a call to conversion: "The kingdom of God has come near. Repent and believe in the Good News." Let's take a closer look at the invitation Christ places on offer.

First, *repent*. Notice that the life, preaching, and mission of Jesus are predicated upon the assumption that all is not well with us. A salvation religion makes no sense if we're all basically fine, if all we need is a little sprucing up around the edges. Christian saints are those who can bear the awful revelation that sin is not simply an abstraction or something that other people wrestle with but a power that lurks and works in them.

Second, *believe in the Good News*. Something here is being brought to completion. What is it? It is the story of Israel itself. Jesus fulfills in his person the entirety of the Old Testament, and this is why his presence is so compelling and why following him is of paramount importance. The Good News is he himself, and it's time to make a decision. When Jesus calls, we have to respond; the time is now.

As we pray this decade, let us contemplate Jesus' proclamation of the coming of the kingdom of God as the inbreaking of a new world, one that commands us to change our way of thinking and acting.

Reflection

(Short Option)

Jesus' first words in the Gospel of Mark are: "The kingdom of God has come near. Repent and believe in the Good News." This proclamation is the inbreaking of a new world, one that changes our way of thinking and acting.

The Our Father

Our Father, who art in heaven,
hallowed be thy name;
thy kingdom come,
thy will be done
on earth as it is in heaven.
Give us this day our daily bread,
and forgive us our trespasses,
as we forgive those who trespass against us;

and lead us not into temptation,
but deliver us from evil.
Amen.

The Hail Mary (ten times)

Hail Mary, full of grace, the Lord is with thee;
blessed art thou among women,
and blessed is the fruit of thy womb, Jesus.
Holy Mary, Mother of God,
pray for us sinners,
now and at the hour of our death.
Amen.

The Glory Be

Glory be to the Father, and to the Son, and to the Holy Spirit;
as it was in the beginning, is now, and ever shall be,
world without end.
Amen.

The Fatima Prayer

O my Jesus, forgive us our sins, save us from the fires of hell;
lead all souls to heaven, especially those most in need of thy mercy.

The Fourth Luminous Mystery: The Transfiguration

Reflection

(Long Option)

Jesus goes up the mountain with Peter, James, and John. This seemingly ordinary man from Nazareth, this brother of theirs, this fellow Israelite, is then transfigured before them, his face shining like the sun and his clothes becoming white as light. The Greek term behind our word "transfiguration" is *metamorphoō* (to go beyond the form that you have). The metamorphosis of a caterpillar comes to mind. This ordinary Jesus—and there is no indication that they have lost sight of who it was—somehow became transformed, elevated, enhanced in his manner of being.

The first thing we notice is that his appearance became more beautiful. One of the classical features of beauty is *claritas* or radiance: his face "shone" and his clothes became "white as light." The proximity of his divinity in no way compromises the integrity of his humanity, but rather makes it shine in greater beauty. These somewhat grubby bodies of ours—whose beauty lasts for a fleeting moment—are destined for a transfigured, elevated beauty.

Secondly, in his transfigured state, Jesus transcends space and time, since he is pictured talking with Moses and Elijah, figures representing the Law and the prophets of the Old Testament. In this world, we are caught in one moment of space and time, but in heaven, we will live in the eternal now of God's life; a higher, richer, more beautiful, and spiritually fulfilling life awaits us.

For this decade, think about how the mystery of the Transfiguration doesn't just reveal who Christ is; it reveals who we sinners are called to become: eternal sons and daughters of the living God.

Reflection

(Short Option)

Jesus goes up the mountain with Peter, James, and John and is beautifully transfigured before them. This reveals not only who Christ is but who we sinners are called to become: eternal sons and daughters of the living God.

The Our Father

Our Father, who art in heaven,
hallowed be thy name;
thy kingdom come,
thy will be done
on earth as it is in heaven.

Give us this day our daily bread,
and forgive us our trespasses,
as we forgive those who trespass against us;
and lead us not into temptation,
but deliver us from evil.
Amen.

The Hail Mary (ten times)

Hail Mary, full of grace, the Lord is with thee;
blessed art thou among women,
and blessed is the fruit of thy womb, Jesus.
Holy Mary, Mother of God,
pray for us sinners,
now and at the hour of our death.
Amen.

The Glory Be

Glory be to the Father, and to the Son, and to the Holy Spirit;
as it was in the beginning, is now, and ever shall be,
world without end.
Amen.

The Fatima Prayer

O my Jesus, forgive us our sins, save us from the fires of hell;
lead all souls to heaven, especially those most in need of thy mercy.

✷

The Fifth Luminous Mystery: The Institution of the Eucharist

Reflection

(Long Option)

Jesus asks his disciples to go into Jerusalem and prepare a Passover supper. The Eucharist is, first, the great meal of fellowship that God wants to establish with his people, the joyful bond in which the divine life is shared spiritually and physically with a hungry world.

However, in a fallen world, this communion is impossible without sacrifice. At the heart of the Passover meal was the eating of a sacrificed lamb in remembrance of the lambs of the original Passover whose blood had been smeared on the doorposts of the Israelites in Egypt. Making his Last Supper a Passover meal, Jesus was signaling the fulfillment of John the Baptist's prophecy that he, Jesus, would be the definitive Lamb of God. This emphasis becomes even clearer when we meditate on the image of the disciples drinking the blood of Jesus from a cup. When someone came to the temple to offer sacrifice, he would cut the throat of the animal, and a priest would catch the victim's blood in a cup before carrying it in for the offering. The implication is clear: Jesus is referring to his own blood being shed for the forgiveness of sins.

After blessing and breaking the unleavened bread of the Passover meal, Jesus pronounced these words: "Take and eat; this is my body." The central claim of the Catholic Church is that Jesus is substantially present under the forms of bread and wine, and that this definitive sacrifice is made sacramentally present at every Mass. His presence is not simply evocative and symbolic, but rather real, true, substantial. If Jesus were simply an ordinary human being, his words would have, at best, a symbolic resonance. But Jesus is God, and what God says, is.

As we pray this final decade, meditate on Christ's institution of the Eucharist as a great meal of fellowship, the definitive sacrifice, and the Real Presence under the forms of bread and wine. The Eucharist is the Lord Jesus himself.

Reflection

(Short Option)

Jesus institutes the definitive sacrifice of the Eucharist at the heart of a Passover meal, making himself really and truly present under the forms of bread and wine.

The Our Father

Our Father, who art in heaven,
hallowed be thy name;
thy kingdom come,
thy will be done
on earth as it is in heaven.
Give us this day our daily bread,
and forgive us our trespasses,
as we forgive those who trespass against us;
and lead us not into temptation,
but deliver us from evil.
Amen.

The Hail Mary (ten times)

Hail Mary, full of grace, the Lord is with thee;
blessed art thou among women,
and blessed is the fruit of thy womb, Jesus.
Holy Mary, Mother of God,
pray for us sinners,
now and at the hour of our death.
Amen.

The Glory Be

Glory be to the Father, and to the Son, and to the Holy Spirit;
as it was in the beginning, is now, and ever shall be,
world without end.
Amen.

The Fatima Prayer

O my Jesus, forgive us our sins, save us from the fires of hell;
lead all souls to heaven, especially those most in need of thy mercy.

Closing Prayers

Hail, Holy Queen

Hail, holy Queen, mother of mercy,
our life, our sweetness, and our hope.
To thee do we cry, poor banished children of Eve;
to thee do we send up our sighs,
mourning and weeping in this valley of tears.
Turn, then, most gracious advocate,
thine eyes of mercy toward us;
and after this, our exile,
show unto us the blessed fruit of thy womb, Jesus.
O clement, O loving, O sweet Virgin Mary.
Pray for us, O holy Mother of God,
that we may be made worthy of the promises of Christ.
Amen.

Concluding Prayer

Let us pray.
O God, whose only begotten Son,
by his life, death, and Resurrection,
has purchased for us the rewards of eternal life,
grant, we beseech thee,
that while meditating on these mysteries

of the most holy Rosary of the Blessed Virgin Mary,
we may imitate what they contain
and obtain what they promise,
through the same Christ our Lord.
Amen.

The Sign of the Cross

In the name of the Father, and of the Son, and of the Holy Spirit.
Amen.

Additional Marian Prayers

The Angelus

Traditionally prayed at 6 a.m., noon, and 6 p.m.

℣. The Angel of the Lord declared unto Mary,
℟. And she conceived of the Holy Spirit.

Hail Mary, full of grace, the Lord is with thee;
blessed art thou among women,
and blessed is the fruit of thy womb, Jesus.
Holy Mary, Mother of God,
pray for us sinners,
now and at the hour of our death.
Amen.

℣. Behold the handmaid of the Lord,
℟. Be it done unto me according to thy Word.

Hail Mary . . .

℣. And the Word was made flesh,
℟. And dwelt among us.

Hail Mary . . .

℣. Pray for us, O holy Mother of God,
℟. That we may be made worthy of the promises of Christ.

Let us pray. Pour forth, we beseech thee, O Lord, thy grace into our hearts: that we, to whom the Incarnation of Christ thy Son was made known by the message of an Angel, may by his Passion and Cross be brought to the glory of his Resurrection. Through the same Christ our Lord. Amen.

✴

The Memorare

Remember, O most gracious Virgin Mary, that never was it known that anyone who fled to thy protection, implored thy help, or sought thy intercession, was left unaided.

Inspired by this confidence I fly unto thee, O Virgin of virgins, my Mother.

To thee do I come, before thee I stand, sinful and sorrowful.

O Mother of the Word Incarnate, despise not my petitions, but in thy mercy hear and answer me.

Amen.

The Litany of Loreto

Lord have mercy.
Christ have mercy.
Lord have mercy. Christ hear us.
Christ graciously hear us.

God, the Father of heaven, *have mercy on us.*

God the Son, Redeemer of the world, *have mercy on us.*
God the Holy Spirit, *have mercy on us.*
Holy Trinity, one God, *have mercy on us.*

Holy Mary, *pray for us.*
Holy Mother of God, *pray for us.*
Holy Virgin of virgins, *pray for us.*
Mother of Christ, *pray for us.*
Mother of the Church, *pray for us.*
Mother of Mercy, *pray for us.*
Mother of divine grace, *pray for us.*
Mother of Hope, *pray for us.*
Mother most pure, *pray for us.*
Mother most chaste, *pray for us.*
Mother inviolate, *pray for us.*

Mother undefiled, *pray for us.*

Mother most amiable, *pray for us.*

Mother admirable, *pray for us.*

Mother of good counsel, *pray for us.*

Mother of our Creator, *pray for us.*

Mother of our Savior, *pray for us.*

Virgin most prudent, *pray for us.*

Virgin most venerable, *pray for us.*

Virgin most renowned, *pray for us.*

Virgin most powerful, *pray for us.*

Virgin most merciful, *pray for us.*

Virgin most faithful, *pray for us.*

Mirror of justice, *pray for us.*

Seat of wisdom, *pray for us.*

Cause of our joy, *pray for us.*

Spiritual vessel, *pray for us.*

Vessel of honor, *pray for us.*

Singular vessel of devotion, *pray for us.*

Mystical rose, *pray for us.*

Tower of David, *pray for us.*

Tower of ivory, *pray for us.*

House of gold, *pray for us.*

Ark of the Covenant, *pray for us.*

Gate of heaven, *pray for us.*

Morning star, *pray for us.*

Health of the sick, *pray for us.*

Refuge of sinners, *pray for us.*

Solace of migrants, *pray for us.*

Comfort of the afflicted, *pray for us.*

Help of Christians, *pray for us.*

Queen of Angels, *pray for us.*

Queen of Patriarchs, *pray for us.*

Queen of Prophets, *pray for us.*

Queen of Apostles, *pray for us.*

Queen of Martyrs, *pray for us.*

Queen of Confessors, *pray for us.*

Queen of Virgins, *pray for us.*

Queen of All Saints, *pray for us.*

Queen conceived without original sin, *pray for us.*

Queen assumed into heaven, *pray for us.*

Queen of the most holy Rosary, *pray for us.*

Queen of families, *pray for us.*

Queen of peace, *pray for us.*

Lamb of God, who takes away the sins of the world,
spare us, O Lord.

Lamb of God, who takes away the sins of the world,
graciously hear us, O Lord.

Lamb of God, who takes away the sins of the world,
have mercy on us.

Pray for us, O holy Mother of God.
That we may be made worthy of the promises of Christ.

Let us pray.
Grant, we beseech thee,
O Lord God,
that we, your servants,
may enjoy perpetual health of mind and body;
and by the glorious intercession of the Blessed Mary, ever Virgin,
may be delivered from present sorrow,
and obtain eternal joy.
Through Christ our Lord.
Amen.

St. Louis de Montfort's Act of Consecration

O Eternal and Incarnate Wisdom! O sweetest and most adorable Jesus! Very God and Very Man, only Son of the Eternal Father, and of Mary ever Virgin! I adore thee profoundly in the bosom and glory of thy Father during eternity; and I adore thee also in the virginal bosom of Mary, thy most worthy Mother, in the time of thine Incarnation.

I give thee thanks, for that thou hast annihilated thyself, in taking the form of a slave, in order to rescue me from the cruel slavery of the devil. I praise and glorify thee, for that thou hast been pleased to submit thyself to Mary, thy Holy Mother, in all things, in order to make me thy faithful slave through her. But alas! ungrateful and faithless slave that I am, I have not kept the promises which I made so solemnly to thee in my Baptism; I have not fulfilled my obligations; I do not deserve to be called thy son, nor even thy slave: and, as there is nothing in me which does not merit thine anger and thy repulse, I dare no more come by myself into the presence of thy Most Holy and August Majesty. It is on this account, that I have recourse to the intercession of thy Most Holy Mother, whom thou hast given me for a mediatrix with thee. It is by her means that I hope to obtain of thee contrition and the pardon of my sins, the acquisition and preservation of Wisdom.

Hail, then, O Immaculate Mary, living Tabernacle of the Divinity, in which the Eternal Wisdom willed to be hidden, and to be adored by angels and by men! Hail, O Queen of heaven and earth, to whose empire everything is subject which is under God!

Hail, O sure refuge of sinners, whose mercy fails to no one! Hear the desires which I have of the Divine Wisdom, and for that end receive the vows and offerings which in my lowness I present to thee.

I, [name], a faithless sinner, I renew and ratify today in thy hands the vows of my Baptism; I renounce forever, Satan, his pomps, and his works; and I give myself entirely to Jesus Christ, the Incarnate Wisdom, to carry my cross after him all the days of my life, and in order that I may be more faithful to him than I have ever been before.

In the presence of all the heavenly court I choose thee this day for my Mother and Mistress. I deliver and consecrate to thee, as thy slave, my body and soul, my goods, both interior and exterior, and even the value of all my good actions, past, present, and future; and I leave to thee the entire and full right of disposing of me, and of all that belongs to me, without exception, according to thy good pleasure, to the greatest glory of God, in time and in eternity.

Receive, O gracious Virgin, this little offering of my slavery, in honor of, and in union with, that subjection which the Eternal Wisdom deigned to have to thy maternity, in homage to the power which both of you have over this little worm and miserable sinner, and in thanksgiving for the privileges with which the Holy Trinity hath favored thee. I protest, that henceforth I wish, as thy true slave, to seek thy honor, and to obey thee in all things.

O admirable Mother! present me to thy dear Son as his eternal slave, so that as he hath redeemed me by thee, by thee he may receive me.

O Mother Mary! get me the grace to obtain the true Wisdom of God, and for that end place me in the number of those whom thou lovest, whom thou teachest, whom thou leadest, and whom thou nourishest and protectest as thy children and thy slaves.

O faithful Virgin, make me in all things so perfect a disciple, imitator, and slave of the Incarnate Wisdom, Jesus Christ thy Son, that I may attain by thy intercession, and by thy example, to the fullness of his age on earth, and of his glory in heaven. Amen.

St. Maximilian Kolbe's Act of Consecration

O Immaculate, Queen of heaven and earth, refuge of sinners and our most loving Mother, God has willed to entrust the entire order of mercy to you. I, [name], an unworthy sinner, cast myself at your feet, humbly imploring you to take me with all that I am and have, wholly to yourself as your possession and property. Please make of me, of all my powers of soul and body, of my whole life, death, and eternity, whatever pleases you. If it pleases you, use all that I am and have without reserve, wholly to accomplish what has been said of you: "She will crush your head," and "You alone have destroyed all heresies in the whole world." Let me be a fit instrument in your immaculate and most merciful hands for introducing and increasing your glory to the maximum in all the many strayed and indifferent souls, and thus help extend as far as possible the blessed kingdom of the Most Sacred Heart of Jesus. For whatever you enter, you obtain the grace of conversion and sanctification, since it is through your hands that all graces come to us from the Most Sacred Heart of Jesus.

℣. Allow me to praise you, O most holy Virgin.

℟. Give me strength against your enemies.

Pope St. John Paul II's Act of Entrustment

O Mother, like the Apostle John,
we wish to take you into our home,
that we may learn from you to become like your Son.
"Woman, behold your son!"
Here we stand before you
to entrust to your maternal care
ourselves, the Church, the entire world.
Plead for us with your beloved Son
that he may give us in abundance the Holy Spirit,
the Spirit of truth which is the fountain of life.
Receive the Spirit for us and with us,
as happened in the first community gathered round you
in Jerusalem on the day of Pentecost.
May the Spirit open our hearts to justice and love,
and guide people and nations to mutual understanding
and a firm desire for peace.
We entrust to you all people, beginning with the weakest:
the babies yet unborn,
and those born into poverty and suffering,
the young in search of meaning,
the unemployed,

and those suffering hunger and disease.
We entrust to you all troubled families,
the elderly with no one to help them,
and all who are alone and without hope.

O Mother, you know the sufferings
and hopes of the Church and the world:
come to the aid of your children in the daily trials
which life brings to each one,
and grant that, thanks to the efforts of all,
the darkness will not prevail over the light.
To you, Dawn of Salvation, we commit
our journey through the new millennium,
so that with you as guide
all people may know Christ,
the light of the world and its only Savior,
who reigns with the Father and the Holy Spirit
forever and ever. Amen.

Notes

Minor style adjustments have occasionally been made on excerpted material for consistency and readability.

I. Daughter of Zion

The New Eve

Poem: Hildegard of Bingen, "O Virga ac Diadema," trans. Nathaniel M. Campbell, *100 Great Catholic Poems*, ed. Sally Read (Elk Grove Village, IL: Word on Fire, 2023), 78–80.

Reflection: Robert Barron, *Catholicism: A Journey to the Heart of the Faith* (New York: Image Books, 2011), 88–89, 90–91.

Reflection: Irenaeus of Lyons, *Against Heresies* 3.22.4, trans. Alexander Roberts and William Rambaut, in Ante-Nicene Fathers, vol. 1, ed. Alexander Roberts, James Donaldson, and A. Cleveland Coxe (Buffalo, NY: Christian Literature, 1885), newadvent.org.

Prayer: Taken from the Office of Readings for the Common of the Blessed Virgin Mary in *The Liturgy of the Hours*, vol. 3, *Ordinary Time: Weeks 1–17* (New York: Catholic Book Publishing, 1975), 1621–1622.

Quote: John Henry Newman, *Meditations and Devotions* (New York: Longmans & Green, 1893), 52.

She Who Is in Labor

Poem: Edith Stein, "Conversation at Night," in *The Collected Works of Edith Stein*, vol. 4, *The Hidden Life: Essays, Meditations, Spiritual Texts*, ed. L. Gelber and Michael Linssen, trans. Waltraut Stein (Washington, DC: ICS, 2014), 133.

Reflection: Barron, *Catholicism*, 90–92.

Reflection: Hans Urs von Balthasar, *Light of the Word: Brief Reflections on the Sunday Readings*, trans. D.D. Martin (San Francisco: Ignatius, 1993), 263–264.

Prayer: Methodius of Olympus, "Oration concerning Simeon and Anna" 5, trans. William R. Clark, in Ante-Nicene Fathers, vol. 6, ed. Alexander Roberts, James Donaldson, and A. Cleveland Coxe (Buffalo, NY: Christian Literature, 1886), newadvent.org.

Quote: *Lumen Gentium* 55, in *The Word on Fire Vatican II Collection*, ed. Matthew Levering (Park Ridge, IL: Word on Fire Institute, 2021), 119.

The Virgin Shall Bear a Son

Poem: Gerard Manley Hopkins, "The Blessed Virgin compared to the Air we Breathe," in *As Kingfishers Catch Fire*, ed. Holly Ordway (Elk Grove Village, IL: Word on Fire Institute, 2023), 67, 69, 75.

Reflection: Robert Barron, *Light from Light: A Theological Reflection on the Nicene Creed* (Park Ridge, IL: Word on Fire Academic, 2021), 65–67.

Reflection: Thomas Aquinas, *The Summa Theologiae of St. Thomas Aquinas, Second and Revised Edition* 3.28.1, trans. Fathers of the English Dominican Province (1920), newadvent.org.

Prayer: *Blessed Art Thou: A Treasury of Marian Prayers and Devotions*, ed. Richard J. Beyer (Notre Dame, IN: Ave Maria, 1996), 105.

Quote: Irenaeus, *Against Heresies* 3.21.6, trans. Alexander Roberts and William Rambaut, ANF 1, ed. Alexander Roberts, James Donaldson, and A. Cleveland Coxe (Buffalo, NY: Christian Literature, 1885), newadvent.org.

The Immaculate Conception

Poem: Paul Claudel, "The Virgin at Noon," trans. Wallace Fowlie, *Poetry* 87, no. 3 (1955): 138–139.

Reflection: Barron, *Catholicism*, 99–101.

Reflection: Newman, *Meditations and Devotions*, 13–15.

Prayer: Padre Pio, *Meditation Prayer on Mary Immaculate* (Charlotte, NC: TAN Books, 2012), 7–8.

Quote: Paul VI, *Marialis Cultus* 57, apostolic exhortation, February 2, 1974, vatican.va.

Sing, O Daughter Zion

Poem: Gerard Manley Hopkins, "May Magnificat," in *As Kingfishers Catch Fire*, 7–11.

Reflection: Barron, *Catholicism*, 113–115.

Reflection: Louis de Montfort, *A Treatise on the True Devotion to the Blessed Virgin*, trans. Frederick William Faber (London: Burns and Lambert, 1863), 99–100.

Prayer: *The Prayers of Catherine of Siena*, ed. Suzanne Noffke (Ramsey, NJ: Paulist, 1983), 156–157, 164–165.

Quote: Joseph Ratzinger, *Daughter Zion: Meditations on the Church's Marian Belief*, trans. John M. McDermott (San Francisco: Ignatius, 1983), 82.

Hymn: Taken from Antiphons in Honor of the Blessed Virgin in *The Liturgy of the Hours*, vol. 1, *Advent Season – Christmas Season* (New York: Catholic Book Publishing, 1975), 1188, 1190.

II. Mother of Jesus

The Spouse of the Spirit

Poem: Condé Benoist Pallen, "Maria Immaculata," in *Dreams and Images: An Anthology of Catholic Poets*, ed. Joyce Kilmer (New York: Boni & Liveright, 1917), 187–188.

Reflection: Bishop Robert Barron, unpublished homily text.

Reflection: John Paul II, Audiences of Pope John Paul II (English) (Vatican City: Libreria Editrice Vaticana, 2014).

Prayer: Francis and Clare, *Francis and Clare: The Complete Works*, trans. Regis J. Armstrong and Ignatius C. Brady, The Classics of Western Spirituality, ed. Richard J. Payne (New York; Mahwah, NJ: Paulist, 1982), 82.

Quote: H.M. Manteau-Bonamy, *Immaculate Conception and the Holy Spirit: The Marian Teachings of St. Maximilian Kolbe*, trans. Richard Arnandez (Libertyville, IL: Franciscan Marytown Press, 1977), 3.

The Mother of God

Poem: Ephrem, "Hymns on the Nativity of Christ in the Flesh," in *100 Great Catholic Poems*, ed. Sally Read, 12–13.

Reflection: Barron, *Catholicism*, 94–99.

Reflection: Cyril of Alexandria, Letter 1, in *Letters 1–50*, trans. John I. McEnerney (Washington, DC: The Catholic University of America Press, 1987), 15, 20–21.

Prayer: Michael Glazier, "Sub Tuum," in *The Modern Catholic Encyclopedia*, 2nd ed., ed. Michael Glazier and Monika K. Hellwig (Collegeville, MN: Liturgical, 2004), 809.

Quote: Ambrose, *Concerning Virginity* 2.2.7, trans. H. de Romestin, E. de Romestin, and H.T.F. Duckworth, in Nicene and Post-Nicene Fathers, Second Series, vol. 10, ed. Philip Schaff and Henry Wace (Buffalo, NY: Christian Literature, 1896), newadvent.org.

She Pondered in Her Heart

Poem: Caryll Houselander, "The Reed," in *100 Great Catholic Poems*, ed. Sally Read, 361.

Reflection: Robert Barron, *Redeeming the Time: Gospel Perspectives on the Challenges of the Hour* (Park Ridge, IL: Word on Fire, 2022), 65.

Reflection: John Eudes, *The Admirable Heart of Mary*, trans. Charles di Targiani and Ruth Hauser (New York: P.J. Kenedy, 1948), 11–12.

Prayer: De Montfort, *True Devotion*, 152.

Quote: De Montfort, *True Devotion*, 186.

A Sword Will Pierce Your Soul

Poem: G.K. Chesterton, "The Queen of Seven Swords," in *The Queen of Seven Swords* (London: Sheed & Ward, 1926), 39–41.

Reflection: Robert Barron, *The Pivotal Players: 12 Heroes Who Shaped the Church and Changed the World* (Park Ridge, IL: Word on Fire, 2020), 104–105.

Reflection: Newman, *Meditations and Devotions*, 69–71.

Prayer: Newman, *Meditations and Devotions*, 329.

Quote: F.X. Lasance, *My Prayer Book: Happiness in Goodness* (New York: Benziger, 1908), 455.

The Role of a Mother

Poem: John Paul II, "Her Amazement at Her Only Child," in *The Place Within: The Poetry of Pope John Paul II*, trans. Jerzy Peterkiewicz (New York: Random House, 1994), 43.

Reflection: Robert Barron, *Proclaiming the Power of Christ: Classic Sermons* (Park Ridge, IL: Word on Fire Institute, 2021), 132–134.

Reflection: Augustine, "Letter 243: To Laetus," in *Letters*, vol. 5, trans. Wilfrid Parsons, in The Fathers of the Church 45, ed. Hermigild Dressler (Washington, DC: The Catholic University of America Press, 1956), 224–225.

Prayer: John Paul II, *Pastores Dabo Vobis* 82, post-synodal apostolic exhortation, March 25, 1992, vatican.va.

Quote: Alphonsus Liguori, *Visits to the Most Holy Sacrament and the Blessed Virgin Mary*, trans. R.A. Coffin (London: Burns and Lambert, 1855), 44.

Hymn: Taken from the Antiphons in Honor of the Blessed Virgin in *The Liturgy of the Hours*, vol. 1, 1189.

III. Mother of the Church

Do Whatever He Tells You

Poem: *The Little Office of the Blessed Virgin Mary*, ed. John E. Rotelle (New York: Catholic Book Publishing, 1988), 24.

Reflection: Robert Barron, *The Priority of Christ: Toward a Postliberal Catholicism* (Grand Rapids, MI: Brazos, 2007), 72–75.

Reflection: *Lumen Gentium* 60–62, in *The Word on Fire Vatican II Collection*, 121–122.

Prayer: Louis-Marie G. de Montfort, *The Secret of Mary: Unveiled to the Devout Soul*, trans. A.P.J. Cruikshank (London: Art and Book, 1909), 52–53.

Quote: Edith Stein, "For the First Profession of Sister Miriam of Little Saint Thérèse, July 16, 1940," in *The Collected Works of Edith Stein*, vol. 4, 106.

Perpetual Virgin

Poem: Jessica Powers, "Total Virgin," in *The Selected Poetry of Jessica Powers*, ed. Regina Siegfried and Robert F. Morneau (Washington, DC: ICS, 1999), 57.

Reflection: Barron, *Light from Light*, 64–65.

Reflection: Jerome, *The Perpetual Virginity of Blessed Mary* 21, trans. W.H. Fremantle, G. Lewis, and W.G. Martley, in Nicene and Post-Nicene Fathers, Second Series, vol. 6, ed. Philip Schaff and Henry Wace (Buffalo, NY: Christian Literature, 1893), newadvent.org.

Prayer: *The Liturgy of St. John Chrysostom*, quoted in John Macquarrie, *Mary for All Christians* (Edinburgh: T&T Clark, 2001), 158.

Quote: Augustine, Sermon 186.1, in *The Faith of the Early Fathers*, vol. 3, ed. and trans. W.A. Jurgens (Collegeville, MN: Liturgical, 1979), 30.

Here Is Your Mother

Poem: Edith Stein, "Juxta Crucem tecum stare!," in Hilda C. Graef, *The Scholar and the Cross: The Life and Work of Edith Stein* (Westminster, MD: Newman, 1955), 209–210.

Reflection: Barron, *Catholicism*, 94, 98–99.

Reflection: G.K. Chesterton, *The Well and the Shallows*, in *Collected Works*, vol. 3 (San Francisco: Ignatius, 1990), 463.

Prayer: Francis, *Lumen Fidei* 60, encyclical letter, June 29, 2013, vatican.va.

Quote: Bernard of Clairvaux, *Hom.* II super "Missus est," 17; Migne, P. L., CLXXXIII, 70-b, c, d, 71-a, quoted in Pius XII, *Doctor Mellifluus* 31, encyclical letter, May 24, 1953, vatican.va.

Mary at Pentecost

Poem: John Paul II, "Embraced by New Time," in *The Place Within*, 49.

Reflection: Robert Barron, *Heaven in Stone and Glass: Experiencing the Spirituality of the Great Cathedrals* (New York: Crossroad, 2000), 13–15.

Reflection: John Paul II, *Redemptoris Mater* 25–26, encyclical letter, March 25, 1987, vatican.va.

Prayer: Vincent Pallotti, *Daily Bread: A Treasury of Prayer from the Pallottines* (Milwaukee, WI: Pallottines, 1991), 24, available at https://udayton.edu/imri/mary/p/prayers-of-saints-to-mary.php.

Quote: John Paul II, *Redemptoris Mater* 24.

Hymn: Taken from the Antiphons in Honor of the Blessed Virgin in *The Liturgy of the Hours*, vol. 1, 1189.

IV. Queen of Heaven

The Assumption

Poem: Alfred Noyes, "The Assumption—An Answer," in *100 Great Catholic Poems*, ed. Sally Read, 385–386.

Reflection: Barron, *Catholicism*, 104–108.

Reflection: Fulton J. Sheen, *The World's First Love: Mary, Mother of God* (San Francisco: Ignatius, 1996), 140.

Prayer: John Paul II, "Solemnity of All Saints," homily, November 1, 2000, vatican.va.

Quote: Robert Bellarmine, Conciones Habitae Lovanii, n. 40, De Assumption B. Mariae Virginis, quoted in Pius XII, *Munificentissimus Deus* 34, apostolic constitution, November 1, 1950, vatican.va.

A Woman Clothed with the Sun

Poem: Thérèse of Lisieux, *The Poetry of Saint Thérèse of Lisieux*, trans. Donald Kinney (Washington, DC: ICS, 2020), 211–222.

Reflection: Barron, *Catholicism*, 108–111.

Reflection: Thérèse of Lisieux, *Story of a Soul: The Autobiography of Saint Thérèse of Lisieux*, trans. John Clarke (Park Ridge, IL: Word on Fire Classics, 2022), 67–68.

Prayer: Joseph Raya and José de Vinck, *Byzantine Daily Worship* (Allendale, NJ: Alleluia Press, 1969), 968–969.

Quote: G.K. Chesterton, "The Towers of Time," in *Collected Works*, vol. 10, *Collected Poetry: Part I* (San Francisco: Ignatius, 1994), 178.

The Warrior Queen

Poem: Dante Alighieri, *Paradise*, ed. and trans. Anthony Esolen (New York: Random House, 2004), 351.

Reflection: Bishop Robert Barron, unpublished homily text.

Reflection: John Paul II, *Redemptoris Mater* 11.

Prayer: Liguori, *Visits*, 114–115.

Quote: Pope Francis, "Holy Mass on the Solemnity of the Assumption of the Blessed Virgin Mary," homily, August 15, 2013, vatican.va.

Hymn: Taken from the Antiphons in Honor of the Blessed Virgin in *The Liturgy of the Hours*, vol. 2, *Lenten Season – Easter Season* (New York: Catholic Book Publishing, 1976), 1649.

The Rosary with Bishop Robert Barron

Robert Barron, *The Rosary with Bishop Robert Barron* (Park Ridge, IL: Word on Fire, 2021).

Additional Marian Prayers

The Angelus: "Angelus," United States Conference of Catholic Bishops, https://www.usccb.org/prayers/angelus.

The Memorare: "Memorare," United States Conference of Catholic Bishops, https://www.usccb.org/prayers/memorare.

The Litany of Loreto: "The Litany of Loreto," vatican.va.

St. Louis de Montfort's Act of Consecration: De Montfort, *Secret of Mary*, 83–86.

St. Maximilian Kolbe's Act of Consecration: Maximilian Kolbe, *Kolbe: Saint of the Immaculata*, ed. Francis M. Kalvelage (New Bedford, MA: Franciscans of the Immaculate, 2001), 247.

Pope St. John Paul II's Act of Entrustment: John Paul II, "Act of Entrustment to Mary" 4–5, October 8, 2000, vatican.va.

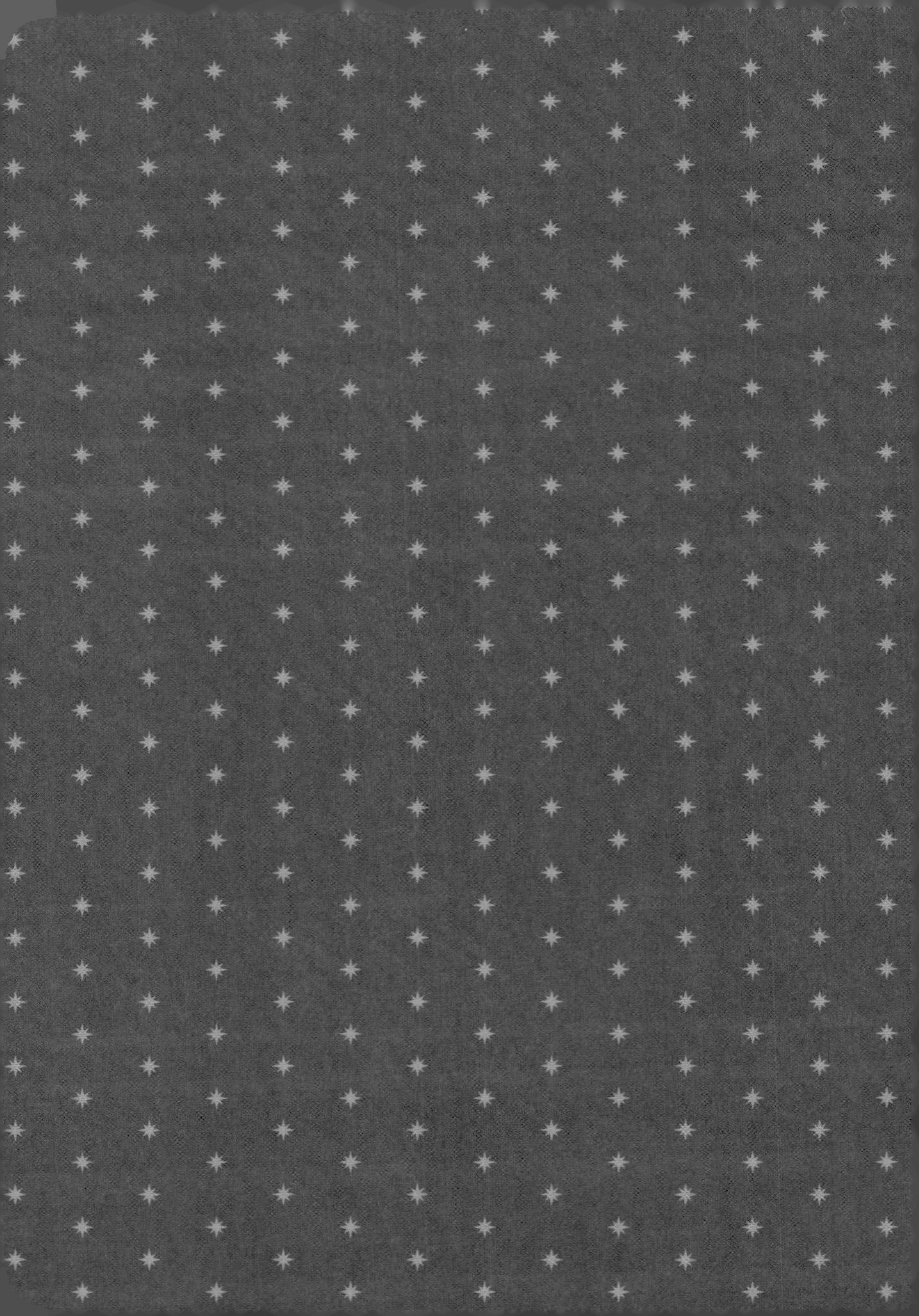